SATs Tests

MATHS READING & GRAMMAR

Year 6

Ages 10–11

KS2

SCHOLASTIC

Scholastic Education, an imprint of Scholastic Ltd
Book End, Range Road, Witney, Oxfordshire, OX29 0YD
Registered office: Westfield Road, Southam, Warwickshire CV47 0RA
www.scholastic.co.uk

© 2017, Scholastic Ltd

4 5 6 7 8 9   8 9 0 1 2 3 4 5 6

British Library Cataloguing-in-Publication Data
A catalogue record for this book is available from the British Library.

ISBN 978-1407-17613-0
Printed in Malaysia

The content in this book has been previously published in Scholastic's SATs Booster Programme.

Authors
Catherine Casey (Maths)
Lesley and Graham Fletcher (Reading and Grammar)

Editorial team
Rachel Morgan, Anna Hall, Kate Pedlar, Audrey Stokes

Series Design
Scholastic Design Team: Nicolle Thomas and Neil Salt

Design
Scholastic Design Team: Neil Salt and Alice Duggan

Cover Design
Scholastic Design Team: Nicolle Thomas and Neil Salt

Cover Illustration
Tomek Giovanis

Illustrations
Tom Heard @ The Bright Agency / Judy Brown /
Moreno Chiacchiera @ Beehive Illustration

Contents

How to use this book

This book will help you to prepare for the National Tests (SATs) which are taken at the end of Key Stage 2 (Year 6). The book is divided into three sections:

Mathematics

Reading

Grammar, Punctuation and Spelling

Each section contains a complete test written in the same style and layout as the National Tests. This will help your child to become familiar with the format of the tests and to know what to expect.

At the end of each section, there is an answer grid where you can record your child's result. This will help you to see which areas your child may need more support in. The comprehensive marking section for each subject provides guidance about what is considered an acceptable answer.

The Mathematics test has three papers:

- **Paper 1:** Arithmetic – these are context-free calculations. Your child will have 30 minutes to answer the questions. There are 40 marks available.
- **Paper 2 and Paper 3:** Reasoning – these are reasoning problems both in and out of context. Your child will have 40 minutes per paper. There are 35 marks available per paper.

The Reading test consists of a combination of texts and questions:

- **Texts** – there are three texts covering different genres. Your child may underline, highlight or make notes.
- **Questions** – your child will need to refer back to the texts but should write their answers in the space provided underneath each question. Your child will have one hour to answer all the questions, *including* reading time. There are 50 marks available.

Be aware that the reading test requires a lot of work to be done in one hour, as it is testing your child's degree of competence – it is not enough to answer questions correctly but slowly.

The Grammar, Punctuation and Spelling test has two papers:

- **Paper 1:** Grammar and Punctuation – this paper contains questions about grammar, punctuation and vocabulary. Your child will have 45 minutes to answer the questions. There are 50 marks available.
- **Paper 2:** Spelling – a transcript consisting of 20 spellings in context is read aloud. Your child must write the spellings in the spaces provided. There are 20 marks available. This paper should take about 15 minutes, but it is not strictly timed.

Practice is vital and every opportunity helps, so don't leave it too late. Using practice tests in the weeks leading up to the National Tests will help to build your child's confidence. Your child will need to develop specific skills such as: reading carefully, leaving difficult questions until the end if they seem too hard, working at a suitable pace and checking their work.

1

MATHS

CONTENTS

Advice for parents and carers

Before the National Tests, provide your child with lots of support and practice.

Step 1:

- Read through the papers in this book so that you know what your child will be doing. You could even try completing them yourself, so you know how difficult they are.

- Let your child take Papers 1 and 2 under examination conditions. Do not provide any help.

- Go through the answers and mark the test together. Talk about which parts of the test your child found difficult.

- Make a list of areas for further revision and encourage your child to practise these areas for two hours each week.

Step 2:

- On a separate occasion, look at Papers 1 and 2 again with your child. Provide extra practice in areas your child struggled with.

- Look at the Sub-strand column in the Paper 3 grid on page 77 to identify similar questions which may cause difficulty. Read through these questions with your child and discuss how they should be answered. Do not reveal the answers.

- Let your child take Paper 3 under examination conditions. Do not provide any help.

- Go through the answers and mark the test together. Talk about the parts of the test your child found difficult. Encourage your child to practise more.

General preparation for the practice tests:

- Make sure that you allow your child to take the practice test in a quiet environment with minimal interruptions or distractions.

- Make sure your child has a flat surface to work on with plenty of space to spread out, and good light.

- Emphasise the importance of reading and re-reading a question and encourage your child to underline or circle any important information.

In the run up to the test:

- Revise and practise on a regular basis.
- Take Papers 1 and 2.
- Mark them with an adult and discuss questions that you found difficult. Make a list of areas for future revision.
- Spend at least two hours each week practising.
- Focus on the areas you are least confident in so that you can improve.
- Take Paper 3 and repeat the steps above.

Just before the test:

- Get a good night's sleep and eat a wholesome breakfast.
- Be on time for school.
- Have all the necessary materials.
- Avoid stressful situations before the test.

During the test:

- Read the questions carefully. Then read them again.
- If a question asks you to 'Show your method' then there will be marks if you get the method correct, even if your answer is wrong.
- If you're struggling with a question, move on and return to it at the end.
- Write as clearly as you can.
- Try to spend the last five minutes checking your work. Do your answers look about right?
- If you have time to spare and have a few questions unanswered, just have a go – you don't lose marks for trying.

Paper 1: Arithmetic instructions

You **may not** use a calculator to answer any questions in this test.

Questions and answers

- You have **30 minutes** to complete this test.
- Work as quickly and carefully as you can.
- Put your answer in the box for each question.

- If you cannot do one of the questions, **go on to the next one**. You can come back to it later if you have time.
- If you finish before the end, **go back and check your work**.

Marks

- The number under each circle at the side of the page tells you the maximum number of marks for each question.
- In this test, long division and long multiplication questions are worth **2 marks** each. You will be awarded 2 marks for a correct answer.
- You may get 1 mark for showing a formal method.

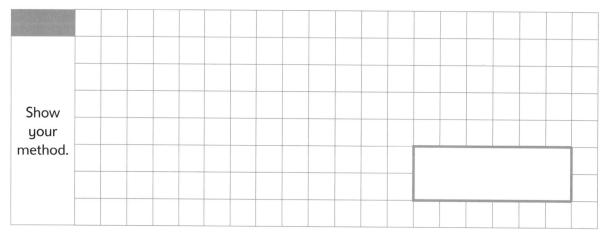

- All other questions are worth **1 mark** each.

		Marks

1. 657 − 329 =

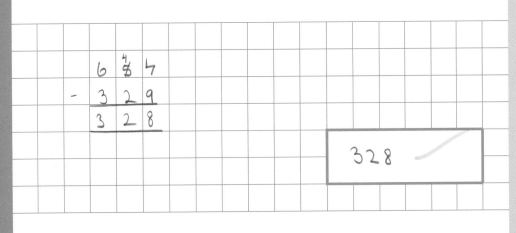

$$
\begin{array}{r}
6 \ \overset{4}{\cancel{5}} \ 7 \\
- \ 3 \ 2 \ 9 \\
\hline
3 \ 2 \ 8
\end{array}
$$

328

 1

2. 88 ÷ 11 =

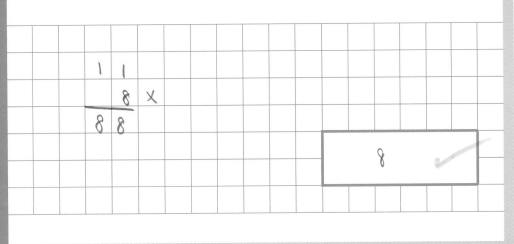

$$
\begin{array}{r}
1 \ 1 \\
\quad 8 \ \times \\
\hline
8 \ 8
\end{array}
$$

8

 1

3. 42,321 − 2000 =

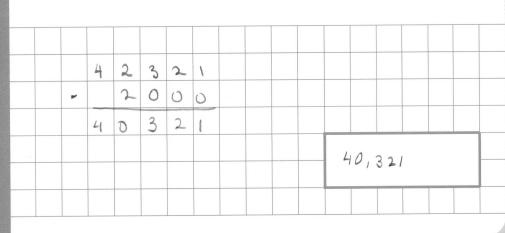

$$
\begin{array}{r}
4 \ 2 \ 3 \ 2 \ 1 \\
- \quad 2 \ 0 \ 0 \ 0 \\
\hline
4 \ 0 \ 3 \ 2 \ 1
\end{array}
$$

40,321

 1

4. 50 × 4 =

Marks

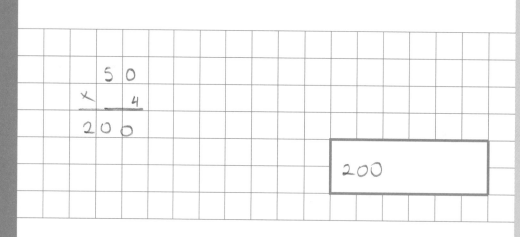

```
      5 0
    ×   4
    2 0 0
```

200

1

5. $\frac{4}{6} - \frac{1}{6} =$

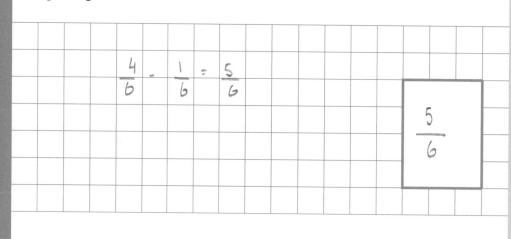

$\frac{4}{6} - \frac{1}{6} = \frac{5}{6}$

$\frac{5}{6}$

1

6. 220 × 4 =

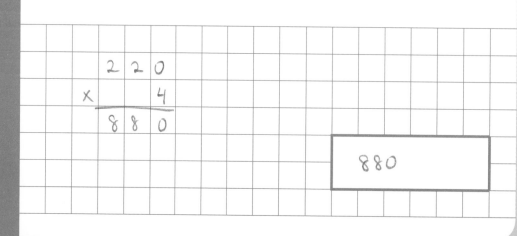

```
      2 2 0
    ×     4
      8 8 0
```

880

1

SCHOLASTIC SATs Tests Maths, Reading and Grammar

7. $14.38 \times 200 =$

Marks

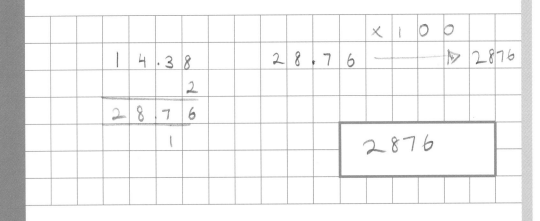

$\times \ 1 \ 0 \ 0$

$1 \ 4 . 3 \ 8$

2

$2 \ 8 . 7 \ 6$

1

$2 \ 8 . 7 \ 6 \longrightarrow \ 2876$

$$\boxed{2876}$$

1

8. $23 \times 8 =$

Marks

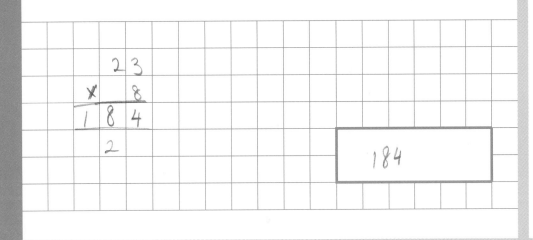

$2 \ 3$

$\times \quad 8$

$1 \ 8 \ 4$

2

$$\boxed{184}$$

1

9. $5^2 =$

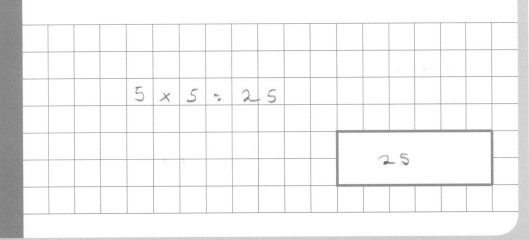

$5 \times 5 = 25$

$$\boxed{25}$$

1

Paper 1: Questions

		Marks
10.	360 ÷ 6 = 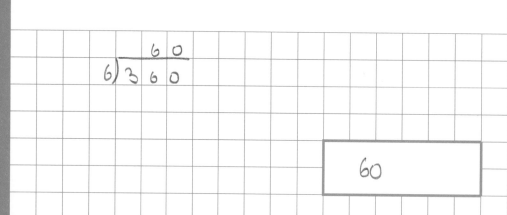	1

$$6 \overline{)360} = 60$$

Answer: 60

11. 3250 + 2364 =

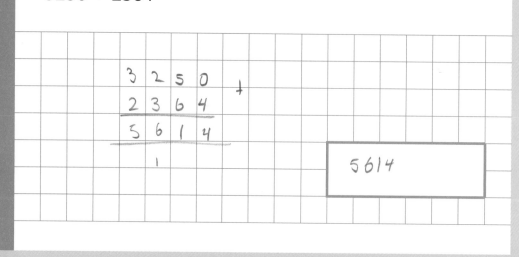

$$\begin{array}{r} 3\,2\,5\,0 \\ 2\,3\,6\,4 \\ \hline 5\,6\,1\,4 \\ {\scriptstyle 1} \end{array} +$$

Answer: 5614

Marks: 1

12. 4 × 2 × 3 =

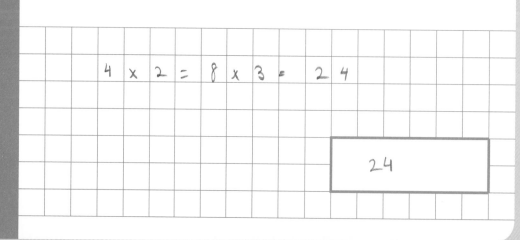

$$4 \times 2 = 8 \times 3 = 24$$

Answer: 24

Marks: 1

13. $27.5 \div 100 =$

Marks

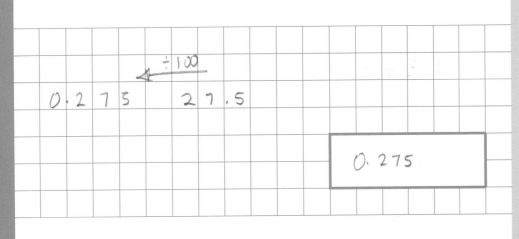

÷100

0.275   27.5

0.275

1

14. 20% of 3300 =

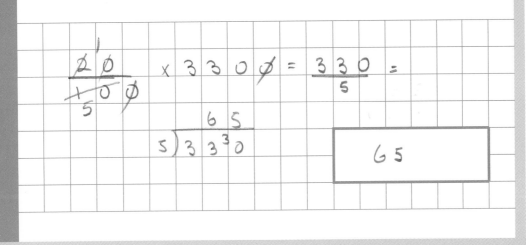

$\frac{20}{50} \times 3300 = \frac{330}{5} =$

65
5)3330

65

1

15. $3200 \div 40 =$

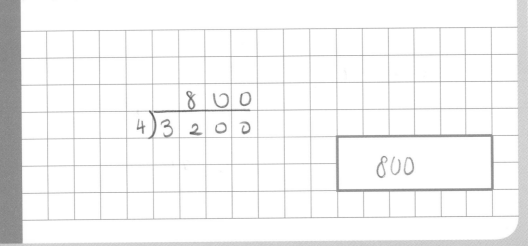

800
4)3200

800

1

		Marks

16. $2\frac{1}{3} - \frac{1}{5} =$

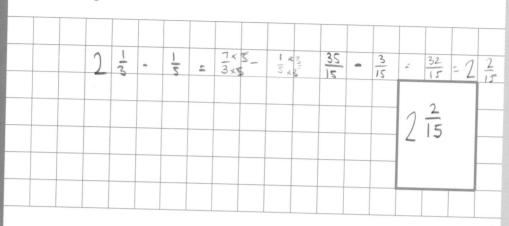

$$2\frac{1}{3} - \frac{1}{5} = \frac{7\times5}{3\times5} - \frac{1\times3}{5\times3} \quad \frac{35}{15} - \frac{3}{15} = \frac{32}{15} = 2\frac{2}{15}$$

$$2\frac{2}{15}$$

1

17. $3^3 =$

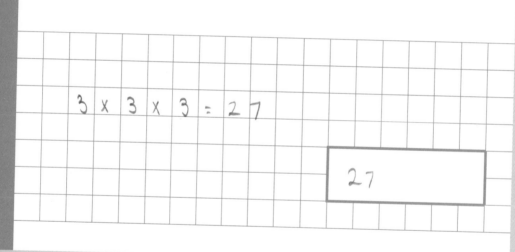

$$3 \times 3 \times 3 = 27$$

$$27$$

1

18. $2.45 \times 5 =$

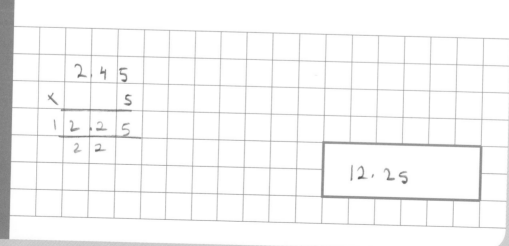

$$
\begin{array}{r}
2.45 \\
\times \quad 5 \\
\hline
12.25 \\
2\ 2 \\
\end{array}
$$

$$12.25$$

1

SCHOLASTIC SATs Tests Maths, Reading and Grammar

19. $\dfrac{3}{5} + \dfrac{3}{5} =$

Marks

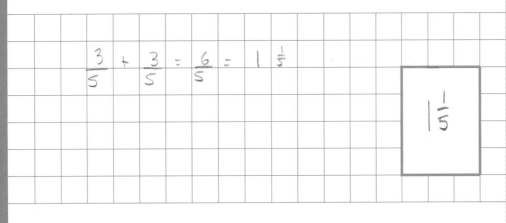

$$\frac{3}{5} + \frac{3}{5} = \frac{6}{5} = 1\frac{1}{5}$$

$1\frac{1}{5}$

1

20. $8234 + 5329 =$

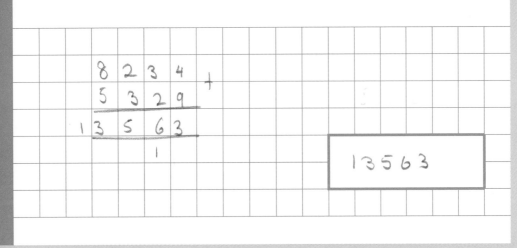

$$
\begin{array}{ccccc}
8 & 2 & 3 & 4 & + \\
5 & 3 & 2 & 9 & \\
\hline
1\ 3 & 5 & 6 & 3 & \\
& & 1 & &
\end{array}
$$

13563

1

21. $3927 \div 7 =$

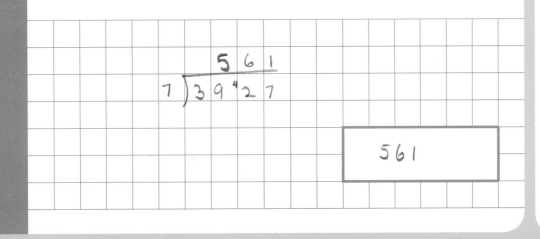

$$7\overline{)3\,9\,^42\,7} = 561$$

561

1

Paper 1: Questions

Marks

22. $\frac{1}{4} \times \frac{1}{5} =$

$$\frac{1}{4} \times \frac{1}{5} = \frac{1}{20}$$

$$\frac{1}{20}$$

1

23. 3.45 − 2.1 =

```
   3 . 4 5
-  2 . 1 0
   1 . 3 5
```

1 . 35

1

24. 28,580 − 8695 =

```
  ¹2⁷8 , ¹4⁷8 ¹8 ⁰0
-      8 , 6  9  5
  1 9   8  8  5
```

19885

1

SCHOLASTIC SATs Tests Maths, Reading and Grammar

25.   10.38 − 8.45 =

Marks

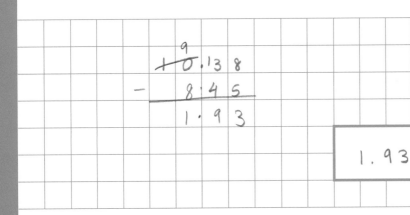

1.93

1

26.   35% of 260 =

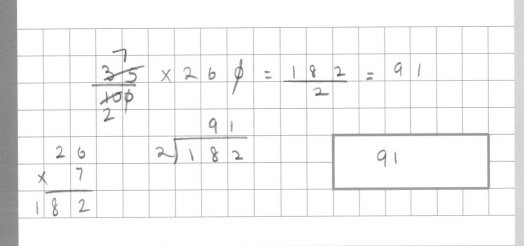

91

1

27.   0.6 × 8 =

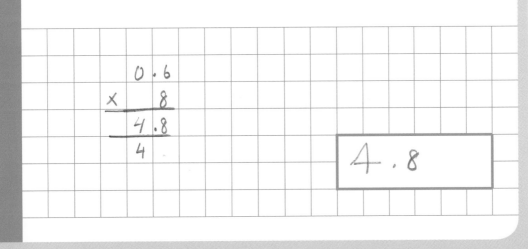

4.8

1

28.

Marks

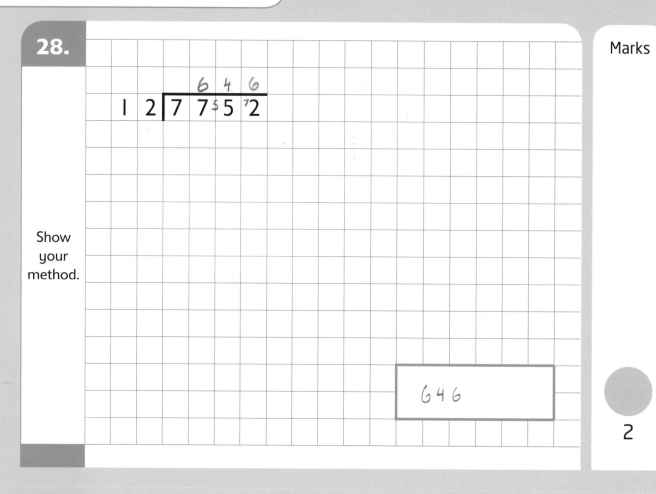

Show your method.

646

2

29.

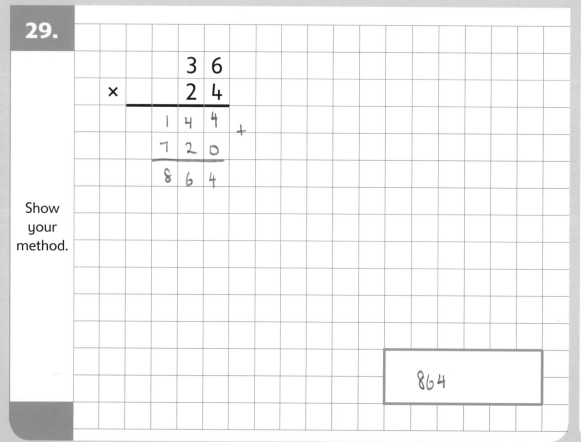

Show your method.

864

2

Marks

30. $\dfrac{5}{6} + \dfrac{1}{2} =$

$\dfrac{5}{6} + \dfrac{1}{2} = \dfrac{5}{6} + \dfrac{1 \times 3}{2 \times 3} = \dfrac{5}{6} + \dfrac{3}{6} = \dfrac{8}{6} = 1\dfrac{2}{6} = 1\dfrac{1}{3}$

$1\dfrac{1}{3}$

1

31. $5 + 24 \div 2 =$

$24 \div 2 = 12 + 5 = 17$

17

1

32. $14 \times 1\dfrac{1}{4} =$

$1\dfrac{1}{4} = \dfrac{5}{4} \times \dfrac{14}{1} = \dfrac{70}{4} = 17\dfrac{2}{4} = 17\dfrac{1}{2}$

$17\dfrac{2}{4} = 17\dfrac{1}{2}$

1

Paper 1: Questions

33. $\frac{3}{7} \div 3 =$

Marks

$$\frac{3}{7} \div \frac{3}{1} = \frac{3^1}{7} \times \frac{1}{3_1} = \frac{1}{7}$$

$\boxed{\dfrac{1}{7}}$

1

34.

$$
\begin{array}{r}
2\,5\,4\,8 \\
\times \quad\quad 3\,6 \\
\hline
1\,5\,2\,8\,8 \\
7\,6\,4\,0 \\
\hline
9\,1\,7\,2\,8 \\
11 \\
\end{array}
$$

Show your method.

$\boxed{91728}$

2

SCHOLASTIC SATs Tests Maths, Reading and Grammar

35. 937,234 + 81,251 =

Marks

```
    9 3 7 , 2 3 4 +
      8 1 , 2 5 1
  1 0 1 6 , 4 8 5
```

1,016,485

1

36.

Show your method.

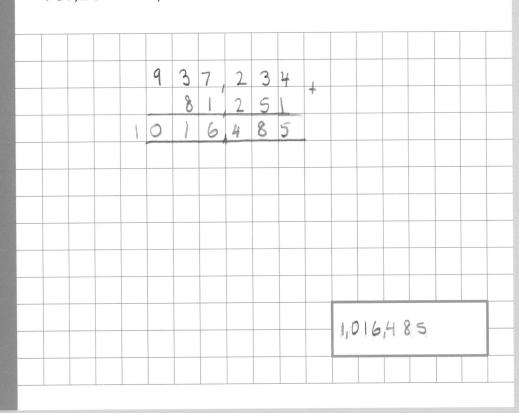

```
        5 6
  7 8 ⌐4 3 6 8
      3 9 0
        4 6 8
```

```
    7 8
  × 5 6
    4 6 8
  3 9 0 0
  4 3 6 8
```

```
  7 8        7 8
  × 5      ×   6
  3 9 0    4 6 8
    4        4
```

56

2

Notes

Paper 2: Reasoning instructions

You **may not** use a calculator to answer any questions in this test.

Questions and answers

- You have **40 minutes** for this test paper.
- Work as quickly and carefully as you can.
- Try to answer all the questions. If you can't do one of the questions, **go on to the next one**. You can come back to it later, if you have time.
- If you finish before the end, **go back and check your work**.

Follow the instructions for each question carefully.

- If you need to do working out, you can use any space on the page – do not use rough paper.

Marks

- Some questions have a method box like this.

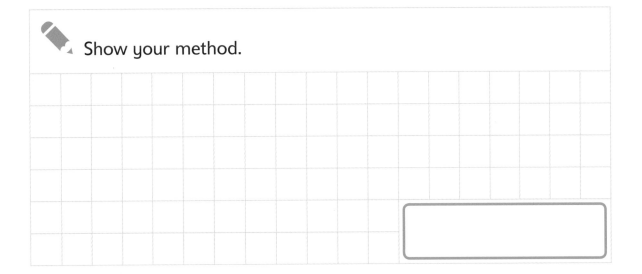

- For these questions you may get a mark for showing your method.
- The number on the right-hand side of the page tells you the maximum number of marks for each question.

Paper 2: Questions

1. Write the number 20,546 in words.

Marks

twenty thousands, five hundred and forty six.

1

2. Put these measurements in order, from smallest to largest.

Marks

55km — 5500 cm

500m — 5000cm

55m — 550 cm

500cm

5.5m → 55 cm

Smallest 5.5 m

500 cm

55 m

500 m

Largest 55 Km

2

Paper 2: Questions

3. The children in Year 6 ran around the school field.

Marks

14m

Not to scale.

25m

How many metres did each child run?

$$\begin{array}{r} 14 \\ \times 25 \\ \hline 70 \\ 28\ 0 \\ \hline 350 \end{array}$$

350   m

1

Marks

4. | Write the missing number.

$$\boxed{139} - 87 = 52$$

$$\begin{array}{r} 52 \\ 87 + \\ \hline 139 \end{array}$$

1

Look at this calculation.

$$\boxed{1178 \times 59 = 69{,}502}$$

| Which inverse calculation could you use to check that this is correct? Tick **one**.

$69{,}502 \times 59 = \boxed{}$

$69{,}502 \div 59 = \boxed{\checkmark}$

$1178 \div 59 = \boxed{}$

$1178 \div 69{,}502 = \boxed{}$

1

Paper 2: Questions

5. Measure angle *x* to the nearest degree.

Marks

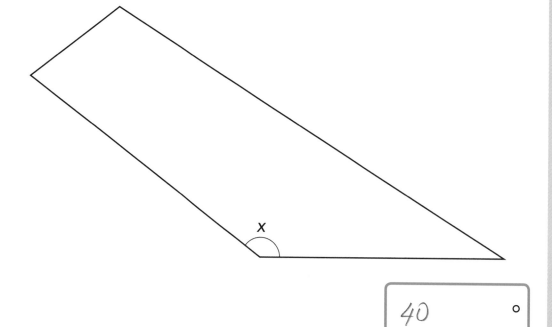

40 °

1

Marks

6. Look at this repeating pattern of shapes.

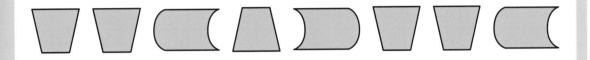

What is the next shape in the pattern? Tick the correct shape.

1

7. Isla's birthday is in 24 weeks and 3 days.

Marks

| How many days is it until Isla's birthday? |

```
 24          168
× 7         +  3
----        -----
168          171
  2            1
```

171   days

1

| How many hours is it until Isla's birthday? |

```
 24         24
×          × 7
---        ------
           168 hrs
```

4104   hours

1

```
 168         24        4032
  24 ×      × 3          72
-----       ----       -----
 672 +       72         4104
3360          1
-----
4032
```

Marks

8. Match each diagram to the percentage that is shaded.

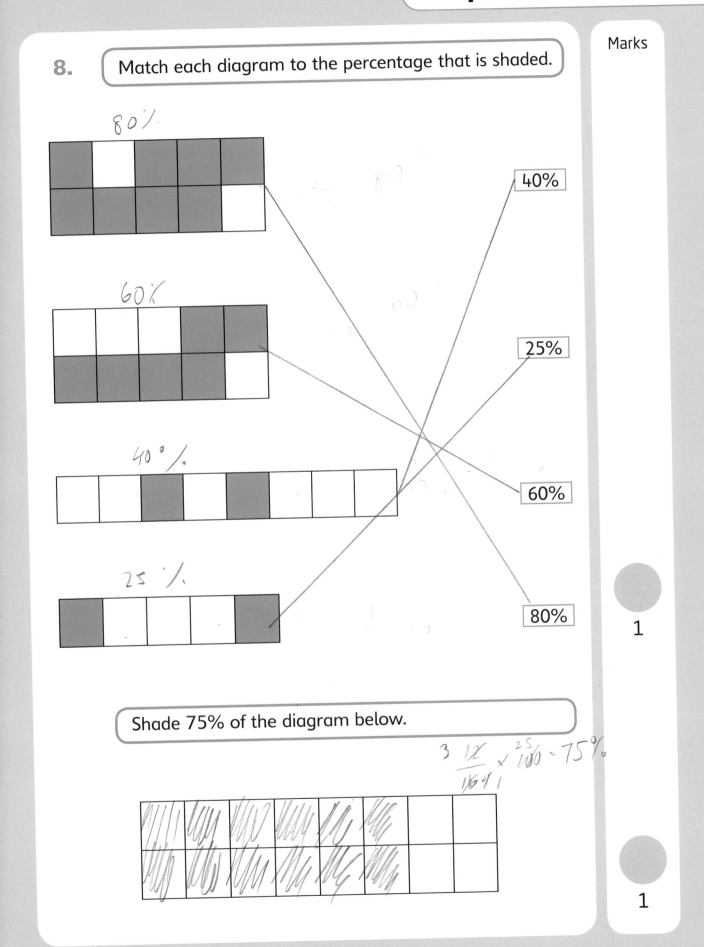

80%

60%

40 °%

25 %

40%

25%

60%

80%

1

Shade 75% of the diagram below.

$3\ \frac{12}{164\ 1} \times \frac{25}{100} = 75\%$

1

Paper 2: Questions

9. | Round these decimals to

Marks

1 decimal place   4.56 =   4.6

2 decimal places   4.567 =   4.57

1

10. Which of these is the net of a square-based pyramid?

Marks

Tick the correct net.

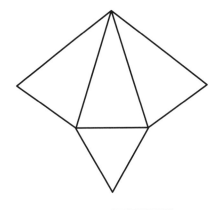

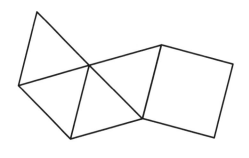

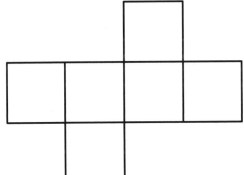

1

Paper 2: Questions

11. The bar graph shows the number of children who went to the school disco from 2011 to 2015.

Marks

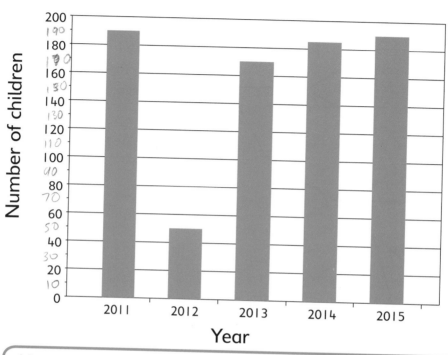

How many children went to the school disco in 2014?

185 children

1

What is the **mean** number of children who attended the school disco from 2011 to 2015?

✏ Show your method.

		1	9	0						
			5	0		7			1 5 7	
		1	7	0			5)7²8³5			
		1	8 ⋅	5						
		1	9⋅	0						
		7	8	5						

157 children

2

■SCHOLASTIC SATs Tests Maths, Reading and Grammar

Marks

12. Alex makes and sells necklaces.

Last month, Alex paid £87 for beads and wire.

She charged £3 for a necklace.

Alex sold 152 necklaces.

How much profit did she make last month?

Show your method.

```
    1 5 2              £ 3 4 ¹4 6 . 0 0
  ×     3            -     8 7 . 0 0
    4 5 6              £ 3 6 9 . 0 0
    1
```

£ 369

2

Paper 2: Questions

13. This is Arun's recipe to make 12 cupcakes.

Marks

190g sugar   190g butter

190g flour   3 eggs

Last Saturday, Arun made 48 cupcakes.

How much flour did Arun use last Saturday?

190
48 ×
1520
7600 +
9120

9120 ÷ 1000 =
9.12

9.12   g

1

On Friday, Arun's class used the recipe. They used 21 eggs.

How many cupcakes did Arun's class make on Friday?

21
× 3
63

63   cupcakes

1

■SCHOLASTIC SATs Tests Maths, Reading and Grammar

Marks

14. $2p + q = 13$

p and q are whole numbers.

Give one possible combination of values for p and q.

p = 5   q = 3

1

Chang says,

"One possible combination is p = 6 and q = 3."

Chang is incorrect.

Explain how you know.

Chang is incorrect because 26 + 3 = 15, 2 x 6 = 12 + 3 = 15 and if you do 2 x 5 + 3 = 13.

1

Marks

15.   Isabel cycled 4km to school and 4km back home each school day.

How many **metres** did Isabel cycle each day?

0.16   m

1

How many **metres** did Isabel cycle to and from school in a week?

0.16
× 7
1.12
1 4

1.12   m

1

■SCHOLASTIC   SATs Tests Maths, Reading and Grammar

16. | Put the fractions in order from smallest to largest.

Marks

$$\frac{4}{9} \, {}^{\times 2}_{\times 2} = \frac{8}{18}$$

$$\frac{1}{6} \, {}^{\times 3}_{\times 3} = \frac{3}{18}$$

$$\frac{3}{10} \, {}^{\times 4}_{\times 4} = \frac{12}{40}$$

$$\frac{6}{8} \, {}^{\times 5}_{\times 5} = \frac{30}{40}$$

$$\frac{4}{5} \, {}^{\times 8}_{\times 8} = \frac{32}{40}$$

| $\frac{1}{6}$ | $\frac{4}{9}$ | $\frac{3}{10}$ | $\frac{6}{8}$ | $\frac{4}{5}$ |

2

Paper 2: Questions

17. Write the missing numbers in the sequence.

Marks

630, 755, [880] , [1005] , 1130, 1255

1

$$
\begin{array}{r}
755 \\
125\, + \\
\hline
880 \\
1
\end{array}
\qquad
\begin{array}{r}
880 \\
125\, + \\
\hline
1005 \\
1
\end{array}
\qquad
\begin{array}{r}
1005 \\
+\ 125 \\
\hline
1130 \\
1
\end{array}
$$

Marks

18.   Five friends go out for dinner.

Main meals cost £10.40 each and desserts cost £3.20.

The friends order five main meals and two desserts.

The friends split the cost equally between them.

How much do they each pay?

✎ Show your method.

```
    1 0 . 4 0          3 . 2 0
X           5                2
  5 2 . 0 0          6 . 4 0
  2

  5 2 . 0 0  +            1 1 . 6 8
     6 . 4 0        5 ) 5 8 . ³4 ⁴0
  5 8 . 4 0
```

£ 11.68

2

Paper 2: Questions

19. Write the missing fractions.

Marks

$$\boxed{\dfrac{1}{3}} \times 3 = 1$$

$\dfrac{1}{1} \div \dfrac{3}{1} = \dfrac{1}{1} \times \dfrac{1}{3} = \dfrac{1}{3}$

$\dfrac{1}{3} \times \dfrac{3}{1} = \dfrac{3}{3}$

1

$$\boxed{\dfrac{8}{32}} \div 8 = \dfrac{1}{32}$$

$\dfrac{1}{32} \times \dfrac{8}{1} = \dfrac{8}{32}$

$\dfrac{8}{32} \div \dfrac{8}{1} = \dfrac{8}{32} \times \dfrac{1}{8} = \dfrac{1}{32}$

1

SCHOLASTIC SATs Tests Maths, Reading and Grammar

Marks

20. A week's holiday costs £345 per person.

There are four people in the family.

The family paid 15% when they booked.

How much more does the family have left to pay?

✎ Show your method.

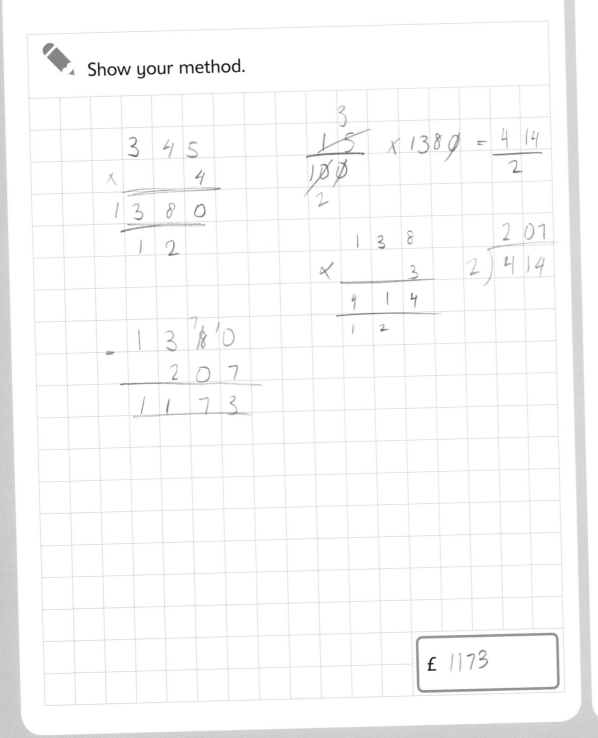

£ 1173

3

Notes

Paper 3: Reasoning instructions

You **may not** use a calculator to answer any questions in this test.

Questions and answers

- You have **40 minutes** for this test paper.
- Work as quickly and carefully as you can.
- Try to answer all the questions. If you can't do one of the questions, **go on to the next one**. You can come back to it later, if you have time.
- If you finish before the end, **go back and check your work**.

Follow the instructions for each question carefully.

- If you need to do working out, you can use any space on the page – do not use rough paper.

Marks

- Some questions have a method box like this.

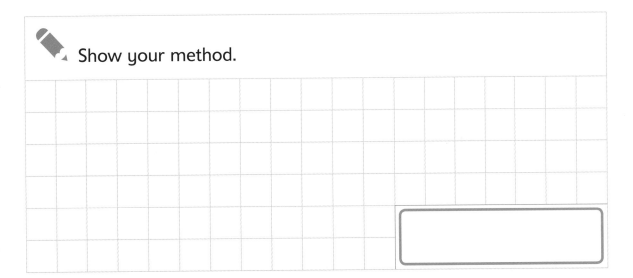

Show your method.

- For these questions you may get a mark for showing your method.
- The number on the right-hand side of the page tells you the maximum number of marks for each question.

Marks

1. The thermometer shows the temperature on Wesley's birthday.

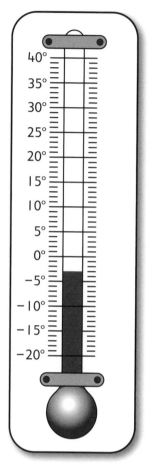

What was the temperature on Wesley's birthday?

-3 °C

1

On Ella's birthday, it was 5°C warmer. What was the temperature?

2 °C

1

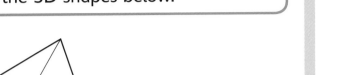

Paper 3: Questions

Marks

2. Write the names of the 3D shapes below.

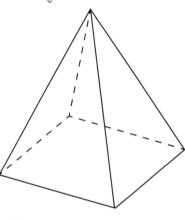

Triangular Prism

Square - Based Pyramid

1

What is the volume of the shape below?

Not to scale.

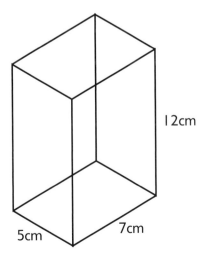

12cm

5cm   7cm

 420   cm³

1

Paper 3: Questions

3. Write the missing numbers in the sequence.

12.5, 16.7, 20.9 , 25.1, 29.3

16.7
- 12.5
4.2

16.7
+ 4.2
20.9

20.9
+ 4.2
25.1

2

4. Write these decimals in the correct places on the number line.

0.3, 0.15, 0.535, 0.36, 0.08

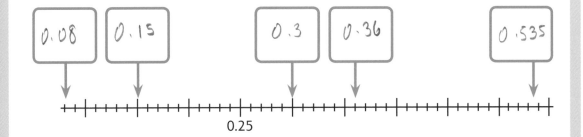

0.25

2

5. Zoe's swimming lesson starts at quarter to 6.

Zoe says her lesson is in 1 hour and 20 minutes' time.

Zoe is correct.

Explain how you know.

Zoe is correct because quarter to 6 is 5:45 and in the ~~watc~~ wha watch is shows 4:25. ~~and~~ In 1 hr it will be 5:25 and if you add 20 minutes to that it is 5:45pm.

1

6. Look at these similar shapes.

Not to scale.

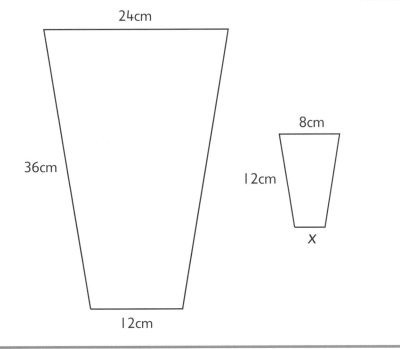

24cm

36cm

12cm

8cm

12cm

x

Calculate the value of x.

42   cm

1

7. On the coordinate grid below, plot and label each of these points.

A: (1, 1)   B: (1, 3)   C: (3, 7)   D: (3, –3)

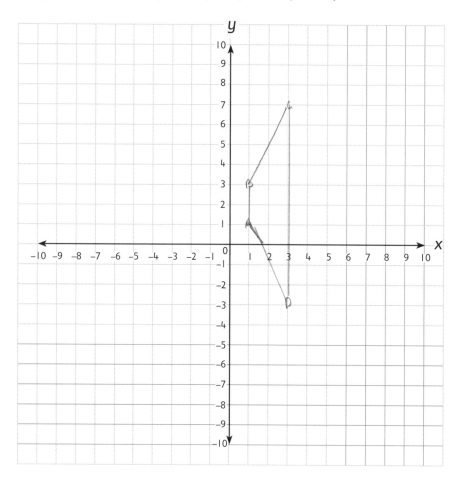

1

Join the points A, B, C and D. What type of quadrilateral is this shape?   *Trapezium*

1

8. Mr Perera cooks pizza.

He uses this formula to calculate how long each pizza will take to cook.

> time for a pizza to cook = diameter of the pizza ÷ 3 + 14

How long would a 27cm pizza take to cook?

2 3   minutes

1

Mr Perera cooks a pizza for 24 minutes.

What is the diameter of the pizza?

3 0   cm

1

9. This is a recipe to make 20 biscuits.

12oz flour

6oz butter

4oz sugar

1oz cocoa

How many grams of butter do you need?

Use 100g = 4oz

| 50 | g |

1

How many ounces of sugar would you need to make 15 biscuits?

| 2 | oz |

1

10. The pie chart shows the type of fruit children chose at playtime.

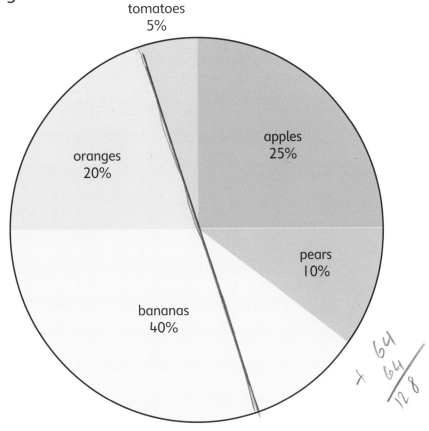

tomatoes
5%

oranges
20%

apples
25%

pears
10%

bananas
40%

There were 32 children who chose oranges.

How many children were there in total?

128 children

1

How many children chose tomatoes?

20 children

1

Paper 3: Questions

11. Look at this number problem.

> What number subtracted from 34,552 equals 12,349?

Tick the algebraic equation that matches the number problem.

$a - 34{,}552 = 12{,}349$ ☐

$12{,}349 - a = 34{,}552$ ☐

$12{,}349 - 34{,}552 = a$ ☐

$34{,}552 - a = 12{,}349$ ☑

1

Look at this number problem.

> What number is three-quarters of 2792?

Tick the algebraic equation that matches the number problem.

$b = (2792 \times 3) \div 3$ ☐

$b = (2792 \div 3) \times 4$ ☐

$b = (2792 \times 4) \div 3$ ☐

$b = (2792 \div 4) \times 3$ ☑

1

12. Measure the largest angle in the triangle below.

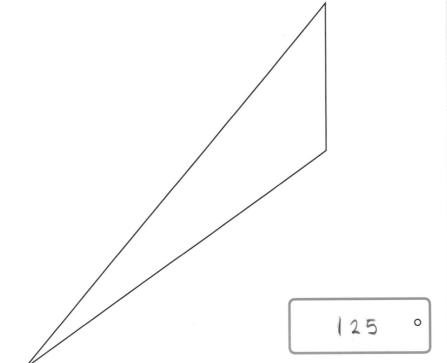

125 °

1

Calculate the size of *y* in the triangle below.

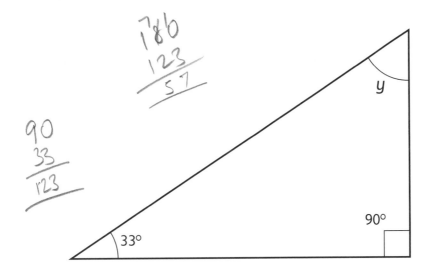

786
123
57

90
33
123

33°

90°

y

57 °

1

Paper 3: Questions

13. Write 64 in Roman numerals.

~~CXIIIIV~~ CXIV

1

SCHOLASTIC SATs Tests Maths, Reading and Grammar

14. Miss Grace chose a number.

She multiplied it by 12, and subtracted 69.

Then she divided by 2.

Her answer was 19.5.

What number did Miss Grace choose?

✏ Show your method.

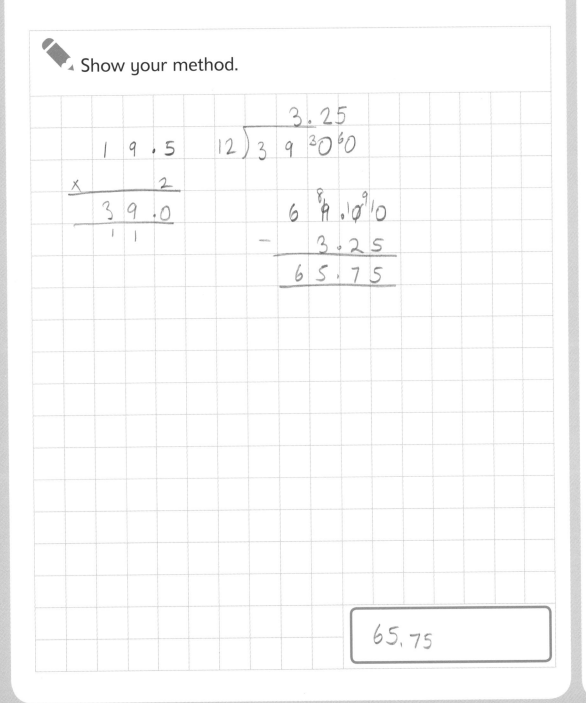

65.75

2

15. What is twenty-three thousand and thirty subtract seventeen thousand, two hundred and thirty-eight?

$$23,000$$
$$30$$
$$17,030$$
$$17,238$$
$$5,792$$

5792

1

16. There were 562 children at a school.

Each child donated 34 books to the new library.

> How many books were in the library?

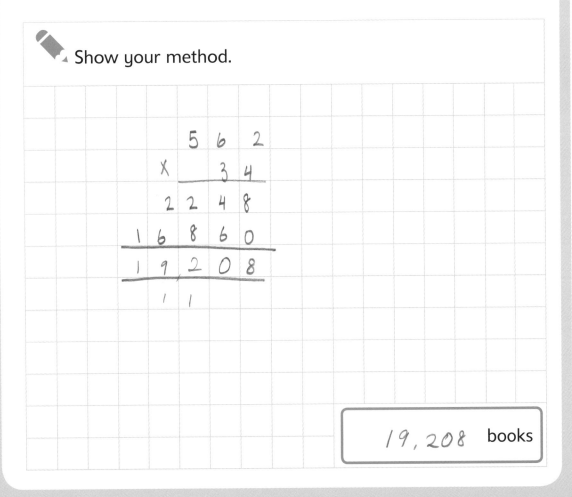

🖉 Show your method.

```
      5 6 2
    x   3 4
    2 2 4 8
  1 6 8 6 0
  1 9,2 0 8
    1 1
```

19,208 books

2

Paper 3: Questions

17. Write the missing whole number.

$$\boxed{8} \times 0.25 = 20$$

1

18. At the school fete, the head teacher sold ice creams.
She sold $\frac{3}{5}$ of the ice creams she had at the start of the fete.

There were 180 ice creams left over.

How many ice creams did the head teacher have at the start of the fete?

🖊 Show your method.

$$\frac{3}{5} \text{ of } 1\ 8\ 0\ =\ 4\ 8$$

$$\begin{array}{r} 1\ \cancel{7}\ \cancel{8}\ 0 \\ -\quad 4\ 8 \\ \hline 1\ 3\ 2 \end{array}$$

132   ice creams

2

19. Write the three missing digits to make this **addition** correct.

$$
\begin{array}{r}
5 \; \boxed{7} \; \boxed{6} \; 1 \\
+ \; \boxed{2} \; 4 \; 7 \; 3 \\
\hline
8 \; 2 \; 3 \; 4
\end{array}
$$

1

SCHOLASTIC SATs Tests Maths, Reading and Grammar

20. The whole school went on a school trip.

It cost a total of £5404 to enter the museum.

The adults' tickets cost a total of £352.

Each child's ticket cost £12.

How many children went to the museum?

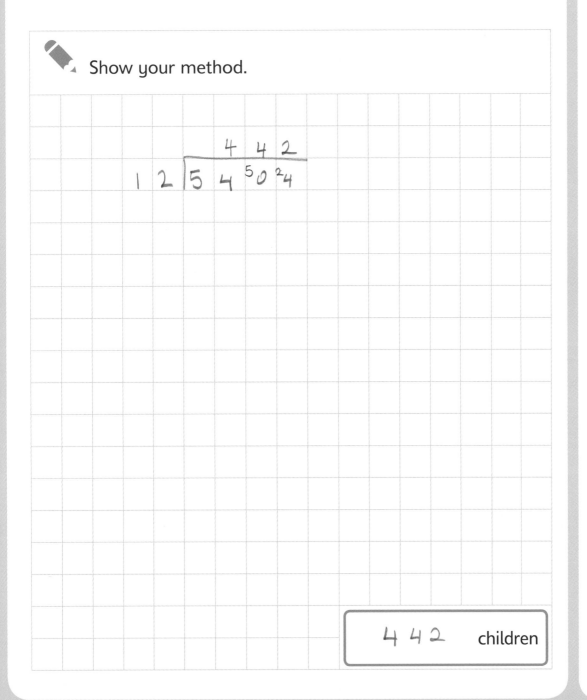

Show your method.

442 children

3

The mark schemes on pages 68–74 provide details of correct answers, including guidance for questions that have more than one mark.

Interpreting answers

The guidance below should be followed when deciding whether an answer is acceptable or not. As general guidance, answers should be unambiguous.

Problem	Guidance
The answer is equivalent to the one in the mark scheme.	The mark scheme will generally specify which equivalent responses are allowed. If this is not the case, award the mark unless the mark scheme states otherwise. For example: $1\frac{1}{2}$ or 1.5.
The answer is correct but the wrong working is shown.	A correct response will always be marked as correct.
The correct response has been crossed (or rubbed) out and not replaced.	Do not award the mark(s) for legible crossed-out answers that have not been replaced or that have been replaced by a further incorrect attempt.
The answer has been worked out correctly but an incorrect answer has been written in the answer box.	Where appropriate, follow the guidance in the mark scheme. If no guidance is given then: ● award the mark if the incorrect answer is due to a transcription error ● award the mark if there are extra unnecessary workings which do not contradict work already done ● do not award the mark if there are extra unnecessary workings which do contradict work already done.
More than one answer is given.	If all answers are correct (or a range of answers are given, all of which are correct), the mark will be awarded unless specified otherwise by the mark schemes. If both correct and incorrect responses are given, no mark will be awarded.

Problem	Guidance
There appears to be a misread of numbers affecting the working.	In general, the mark should not be awarded. However, in two-mark questions that have a working mark, award one mark if the working is applied correctly using the misread numbers, provided that the misread numbers are comparable in difficulty to the original numbers. For example, if '243' is misread as '234', both numbers may be regarded as comparable in difficulty.
No answer is given in the expected place, but the correct answer is given elsewhere.	Where an understanding of the question has been shown, award the mark. In particular, where a word or number response is expected, a child may meet the requirement by annotating a graph or labelling a diagram elsewhere in the question.

Q.	Answers	Marks
1	328	1
2	8	1
3	40,321	1
4	200	1
5	$\frac{3}{6}$ or $\frac{1}{2}$	1
6	880	1
7	2876	1
8	184	1
9	25	1
10	60	1
11	5614	1
12	24	1
13	0.275	1
14	660	1
15	80	1
16	$\frac{32}{15}$ or $2\frac{2}{15}$	1
17	27	1
18	12.25	1
19	$\frac{6}{5}$ or $1\frac{1}{5}$	1
20	13,563	1
21	561	1
22	$\frac{1}{20}$	1
23	1.35	1
24	19,885	1
25	1.93	1
26	91	1
27	4.8	1
28	**Award 2 marks** for the correct answer: 646 **Award 1 mark** for the formal written method for long division but with one arithmetical error. **Do not award** any marks if no final answer has been written in the calculation.	2

Q	Answers	Marks
29	**Award 2 marks** for the correct answer: 864 **Award 1 mark** for the formal written method for long multiplication but with one arithmetical error. **Do not award** any marks if there is an error in the place value of the multiplication or if no final answer has been written in the calculation.	2
30	$\frac{8}{6}$ or $1\frac{2}{6}$ or $\frac{4}{3}$ or $1\frac{1}{3}$	1
31	17	1
32	$\frac{70}{4}$ or $17\frac{2}{4}$ or $17\frac{1}{2}$	1
33	$\frac{1}{7}$ or $\frac{3}{21}$	1
34	**Award 2 marks** for the correct answer: 91,728 **Award 1 mark** for the formal written method for long multiplication but with one arithmetical error. **Do not award** any marks if there is an error in the place value of the multiplication or if no final answer has been written in the calculation.	2
35	1,018,485	1
36	**Award 2 marks** for the correct answer: 56 **Award 1 mark** for the formal written method for long division but with one arithmetical error. **Do not award** any marks if no final answer has been written in the calculation.	2
	Total	40

Mathematics mark scheme: Paper 2

Q	Answers	Marks
1	twenty thousand, five hundred and forty-six	1
2	500cm, 5.5m, 55m, 500m, 55km **Award 2 marks** for the correct answer. **Award 1 mark** for three answers in the correct order.	2
3	78m	1
4	139 69,502 ÷ 59 =	1 1
5	143° (allow answers in the range: 141°–145°)	1
6		1
7	171 days 4104 hours	1 1
8	**Award 1 mark** for all diagrams and percentages matched correctly. **Award 1 mark** for any 12 parts of the rectangle shaded.	1 1

Q	Answers	Marks
9	4.6	I
	4.57	
10		I
11	185 children (allow answers between 183 and 187)	I
	Award 2 marks for the correct answer: 157 children (allow answers between 155 and 159)	2
	Award I mark for evidence of an appropriate method, for example: adding all the numbers of children and dividing by 5.	
12	**Award 2 marks** for the correct answer: £369	2
	Award I mark for an appropriate method but with one arithmetical error. Do not award any marks if there is an error in the place value of the multiplication.	
13	760g	I
	84 cupcakes	I
14	Award I mark for any of the following combinations.	I

p	6	5	4	3	2	I
q	I	3	5	7	9	11

14	Award I mark for an explanation that shows that when $p = 6$ and $q = 3$, then $2p + q = (2 \times 6) + 3 = 15$, which is greater than 13 or that shows that when $p = 6$, then the value of q must be I in order for $2p + q = 13$.	I
15	8000m	I
	40,000m	I
16	$\frac{1}{6}, \frac{3}{10}, \frac{4}{9}, \frac{6}{8}, \frac{4}{5}$	2
	Award 2 marks for the correct answer:	
	Award I mark for three fractions in the correct position.	
17	630, 755, **880, 1005,** 1130, 1255	I
18	**Award 2 marks** for the correct answer: £11.68	2
	Award I mark for evidence of an appropriate method, for example: 10.40 × 5 = 52 3.20 × 2 = 6.40 52 + 6.40 = 58.40 58.40 ÷ 5	

Q	Answers	Marks
19	$\frac{1}{3}$	1
	$\frac{1}{4}$	1
20	**Award 3 marks** for the correct answer: £1173	3
	Award 2 marks for evidence of an appropriate method that contains only one arithmetical error or evidence of a formal method for long multiplication for 15% of £1,380 (1380 × 0.15).	
	Award 1 mark for evidence of an appropriate method, that contains more than one arithmetical error.	
	Total	35

★SCHOLASTIC SATs Tests Maths, Reading and Grammar

Q.	Answers	Marks
1	−3°C	1
	2°C	1
2	triangular prism square-based pyramid	1
	420cm³	1
3	12.5, 16.7, **20.9**, 25.1, **29.3** **Award 2 marks** for the correct answer. **Award 1 mark** for one correct answer.	2
4	**Award 2 marks** for all decimals correctly placed. 0.08 0.15 0.3 0.36 0.535 0.25 **Award 1 mark** for three decimals correctly placed.	2
5	**Award 1 mark** for an explanation that shows that adding 1 hour and 20 minutes to the time shown on the watch (25 minutes past 4) gives 45 minutes past 5, which is the same as quarter to 6.	1
6	4cm	1
7		1
	Trapezium	1

Q	Answers	Marks
8	23 minutes	1
	30cm	1
9	150g	1
	3oz	1
10	160 children	1
	8 children	1
11	$34{,}552 - a = 12{,}349$	1
	$b = (2792 \div 4) \times 3$	1
12	125° (Allow answers between 123° and 127°)	1
	57°	1
13	LXIV	1
14	**Award 2 marks** for the correct answer: 9	2
	Award 1 mark for evidence of the correct operations in the correct order: × 2, + 69, ÷ 12.	
15	5792 or five thousand, seven hundred and ninety-two	1
16	**Award 2 marks** for the correct answer: 19,108	2
	Award 1 mark for the formal written method for long multiplication but with one arithmetical error.	
	Do not award any marks if there is an error in the place value of the multiplication.	
17	80	1
18	**Award 2 marks** for the correct answer: 450 ice creams	2
	Award 1 mark for evidence of an appropriate method, for example: $\frac{2}{5} = 180$ $180 \div 2 = 90$ $90 \times 5 = 450$	
19	$\begin{array}{r} 5\,\mathbf{7}\,6\,1 \\ +\ \underline{\mathbf{2}\,4\,7\,3} \\ 8\,2\,3\,4 \end{array}$	1
20	**Award 3 marks** for the correct answer: 421 children	3
	Award 2 marks for evidence of an appropriate method that contains only one arithmetical error or evidence of a formal method for long division for 5052 ÷ 12.	
	Award 1 mark for evidence of an appropriate method that contains more than one arithmetical error.	
	Total	35

SCHOLASTIC SATs Tests Maths, Reading and Grammar

Paper 1: Answer grid

Question		Possible marks	Actual marks	Question		Possible marks	Actual marks
1	657 − 329	1		19	$\frac{3}{5} + \frac{3}{5}$	1	
2	88 ÷ 11	1		20	8234 + 5329	1	
3	42,321 − 2000	1		21	3927 ÷ 7	1	
4	50 × 4	1		22	$\frac{1}{4} \times \frac{1}{5}$	1	
5	$\frac{4}{6} - \frac{1}{6}$	1		23	3.45 − 2.1	1	
6	220 × 4	1		24	28,580 − 8695	1	
7	14.38 × 200	1		25	10.38 − 8.45	1	
8	23 × 8	1		26	35% of 260	1	
9	5^2	1		27	0.6 × 8	1	
10	360 ÷ 6	1		28	1 2 $\overline{)7\ 7\ 5\ 2}$	2	
11	3250 + 2364	1		29	36 × 24	2	
12	4 × 2 × 3	1		30	$\frac{5}{6} + \frac{1}{2}$	1	
13	27.5 ÷ 100	1		31	5 + 24 ÷ 2	1	
14	20% of 3300	1		32	$14 \times 1\frac{1}{4}$	1	
15	3200 ÷ 40	1		33	$\frac{3}{7} \div 3$	1	
16	$2\frac{1}{3} - \frac{1}{5}$	1		34	2548 × 36	2	
17	3^3	1		35	937,234 + 81,251	1	
18	2.45 × 5	1		36	7 8 $\overline{)4\ 3\ 6\ 8}$	2	
					Total	**40**	

Mathematics Year 6

Paper 2: Answer grid

Q	Strand	Sub-strand	Possible marks	Actual marks
1	Number and place value	Read, write, order and compare numbers	1	
2	Measurement	Compare, describe and order measures	2	
3	Measurement	Perimeter, area	1	
4	Calculations	Estimate, use inverses and check	2	
5	Geometry	Angles – measuring and properties	1	
6	Geometry	Patterns	1	
7	Measurement	Telling time, ordering time, duration and units of time	2	
8	Fractions, decimals, %	Fractions / decimals / percentage equivalence	2	
9	Fractions, decimals, %	Rounding decimals	1	
10	Geometry	Draw and make shapes and relate 2D to 3D shapes (including nets)	1	
11	Statistics	Interpret and represent data Mean average	3	
12	Measurement	Money Solve problems (money; length; mass / weight; capacity / volume)	2	
13	Ratio and proportion	Relative sizes, similarity	2	
14	Algebra	Enumerate all possibilities of combinations of two variables	2	
15	Measurement	Convert between metric units Solve problems (money; length; mass / weight; capacity / volume)	2	
16	Fractions, decimals, %	Comparing and ordering fractions	2	
17	Algebra	Generate and describe linear number sentences	1	
18	Measurement	Money Solve problems (money; length; mass / weight; capacity / volume)	2	
19	Fractions, decimals, %	Multiply / divide fractions	2	
20	Fractions, decimals, %	Solve problems with percentages	3	
		Total	35	

SATs Tests Maths, Reading and Grammar

Q	Strand	Sub-strand	Possible marks	Actual marks
1	Measurement Number and place value	Estimate, measure and read scales Negative numbers	2	
2	Geometry Measurement	Recognise and name common shapes Volume	2	
3	Algebra	Generate and describe linear number sequences	2	
4	Fractions, decimals, %	Compare and order decimals	2	
5	Measurement	Telling time, ordering time, duration and units of time	1	
6	Ratio and proportion	Scale factors	1	
7	Geometry	Coordinates Describe properties and classify shapes	2	
8	Algebra	Simple formulae expressed in words	2	
9	Measurement	Convert metric / imperial	2	
10	Statistics	Interpret and represent data Solve problems involving data	2	
11	Algebra	Missing number problems expressed in algebra	2	
12	Geometry	Angles – measuring and properties	2	
13	Number and place value	Roman numerals	1	
14	Calculations	Solve problems (commutative, associative, distributive and all four operations)	2	
15	Number and place value Calculations	Read, write, order and compare numbers Add / subtract using written methods	1	
16	Calculations	Multiply / divide using written methods	2	
17	Fractions, decimals, %	Multiply / divide decimals	1	
18	Ratio and proportion	Unequal sharing and grouping	2	
19	Calculations	Add / subtract using written methods	1	
20	Measurement	Money Solve problems (money; length; mass / weight; capacity / volume)	3	
		Total	35	

The test content is divided into strands and sub-strands. These are listed for Papers 2 and 3 on pages 76–77 to allow tracking of difficulties. A small number of aspects are not tested, where practical equipment (such as containers) would be required.

Strand	Sub-strand
Number and place value	counting (in multiples)
	read, write, order and compare numbers
	place value; Roman numerals
	identify, represent and estimate; rounding
	negative numbers
	number problems
Addition, subtraction, multiplication and division (calculations)	add/subtract mentally
	add/subtract using written methods
	estimates, use inverses and check
	add/subtract to solve problems
	properties of numbers (multiples, factors, primes, squares and cubes)
	multiply/divide mentally
	multiply/divide using written methods
	solve problems (commutative, associative, distributive and all four operations)
	order of operations
Fractions	recognise, find, write, name and count fractions
	equivalent fractions
	compare and order fractions
	add/subtract fractions
	multiply/divide fractions
	fraction/decimal equivalence
	rounding decimals
	compare and order decimals
	multiply/divide decimals
	solve problems with fractions and decimals
	fraction/decimal/percentage equivalence
	solve problems with percentages

Strand	Sub-strand
Ratio and proportion	relative sizes, similarity
	use of percentages for comparison
	scale factors
	unequal sharing and grouping
Algebra	missing number problems expressed in algebra
	simple formulae expressed in words
	generate and describe linear number sequences
	number sentences involving two unknowns
	enumerate all possibilities of combinations of two variables
Measurement	compare, describe and order measures
	estimate, measure and read scales
	money
	telling time, ordering time, duration and units of time
	convert between metric units
	convert metric/imperial
	perimeter, area
	volume
	solve problems (money; length; mass/weight; capacity/volume)
Geometry – properties of shapes	recognise and name common shapes
	describe properties and classify shapes
	draw and make shapes and relate 2D and 3D shapes (including nets)
	angles – measuring and properties
	parts of a circle including radius, diameter and circumference
Geometry – position and direction	patterns
	describe position, direction and movement
	coordinates
Statistics	interpret and represent data
	solve problems involving data
	mean average

Formal written methods

The following guidance, showing examples of formal written methods, is taken directly from the National Curriculum guidelines. These methods may not be used in all schools and any formal written method, which is preferred by the school and which gives the correct answer, should be acceptable.

Long multiplication

24×16 becomes

```
      ²
    2   4
×   1   6
─────────
2   4   0
1   4   4
─────────
3   8   4
```

Answer: 384

124×26 becomes

```
    ¹   ²
1   2   4
×       2   6
─────────────
2   4   8   0
    7   4   4
─────────────
3   2   2   4
    ¹   ¹
```

Answer: 3224

124×26 becomes

```
    ¹   ²
1   2   4
×       2   6
─────────────
    7   4   4
2   4   8   0
─────────────
3   2   2   4
    ¹   ¹
```

Answer: 3224

Short division

$98 \div 7$ becomes

```
    1   4
  ┌────────
7 │ 9  ²8
```

Answer: 14

$432 \div 5$ becomes

```
      8   6   r2
  ┌──────────────
5 │ 4   3  ³2
```

Answer: 86 remainder 2

$496 \div 11$ becomes

```
       4   5   r1
   ┌───────────────
11 │ 4   9  ⁵6
```

Answer: $45\frac{1}{11}$

Long division

$432 \div 15$ becomes

```
        2   8   r12
   ┌─────────────
15 │ 4   3   2
     3   0   0
   ──────────
     1   3   2
     1   2   0
   ──────────
         1   2
```

Answer: 28 remainder 12

$432 \div 15$ becomes

```
        2   8
   ┌─────────────
15 │ 4   3   2
     3   0   0      15 × 20
   ──────────
     1   3   2
     1   2   0      15 × 8
   ──────────
         1   2
```

$\frac{\cancel{12}}{\cancel{15}} = \frac{4}{5}$

Answer: $28\frac{4}{5}$

$432 \div 15$ becomes

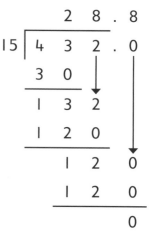

Answer: 28.8

SCHOLASTIC   SATs Tests Maths, Reading and Grammar

The mark that your child gets in the test paper will be known as the 'raw score' (for example, '28' in 28/40). The raw score will be converted to a scaled score and children achieving a scaled scored of 100 or more will achieve the National Standard in that subject. The DfE has introduced a conversion table to create a 'scaled score' for the tests. A 'scaled score' will enable results to be reported consistently year-on-year.

The guidance in the table below shows the marks (raw score) that children need to achieve to reach the National Standard. This should be treated as a guide only, as the number of marks may vary. You can also find up-to-date information about scaled scores on our website: www.scholastic.co.uk/nationaltests

Marks achieved	Standard
0–59	Has not met the National Standard in Mathematics for Key Stage 2.
60–110	Has met the National Standard in Mathematics for Key Stage 2.

Notes

2

READING

CONTENTS

Advice for parents and carers

In the run up to the National Tests, provide your child with lots of support and practice.

Before the test:

- Read through the test so that you know what your child will be doing. You could even try completing it yourself, so you know how difficult it is.

- Let your child take the test under examination conditions (one hour to answer all the questions *including* reading time). Do not provide any help.

- Go through the answers and mark the test together. Talk about which parts of the test your child found difficult.

- Make a list of areas for further revision and encourage your child to practise these areas for two hours each week.

General preparation for the practice tests:

- Make sure that you allow your child to take the practice test in a quiet environment with minimal distractions.

- Make sure your child has a flat surface to work on with plenty of space to spread out, and good light.

- Emphasise the importance of reading and re-reading a question and encourage your child to underline or circle any important information.

- Most of the marks on the tests come from questions that ask your child to retrieve information or make inferences. Spend more time practising these.

In the run up to the test:

- Revise and practise on a regular basis.
- Take the practice test.
- Mark it with an adult and discuss questions that you found difficult. Make a list of areas for future revision.
- Spend at least two hours each week practising.
- Focus on the areas you are least confident in so that you can improve.

Just before the test:

- Get a good night's sleep and eat a wholesome breakfast.
- Be on time for school.
- Have all the necessary materials.
- Avoid stressful situations before the test.

During the test:

- Read the questions carefully. Then read them again.
- Circle or underline any important information in the question.
- If you're struggling with a question, move on and return to it at the end.
- Write as clearly as you can.
- Use every minute of the test time. If you've finished, check your answers.

The legend of Robin Hood

One of the most endearing and enduring of all English legends is the one about Robin Hood. Perhaps it is not surprising. He was brave and dashing. He fought against evil. He stole from the rich and gave to the poor. Or did he?

What was he like?

Robin Hood is such a popular figure that he has been portrayed in several Hollywood movies, in books and on television. In all of these he is seen as a hero. He dressed in 'Lincoln Green'; led a band of 'Merry Men'; and fought for justice. Despite all of this, he was an outlaw and his band of followers was thought to be 100 strong. How would we feel nowadays if a criminal gang of that size was hiding in Sherwood Forest?

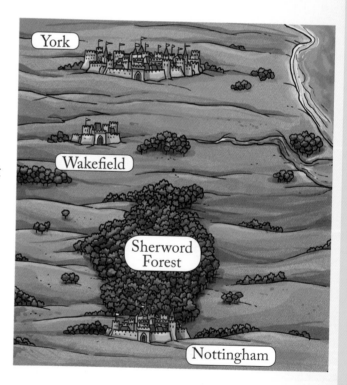

Who was the real Robin Hood?

It would appear that nobody knows. Most accounts agree that he lived during the time of Richard the Lionheart and King John. This would date him as living in about 1190. That's about as far as the agreement goes. Some people think he was the Earl of Huntingdon, others think he was Robin of Loxley. He is also known as Robin Hood of Wakefield and Robin Hood of York. To confuse things more, he could have come from North Yorkshire or Doncaster. There have to be reasons why Robin Hood's Bay and Robin Hood airport are both named after him.

Why don't we know?

If Robin Hood was real, he lived over 800 years ago. In those days, few people could write, so stories were passed down by word of mouth. That means that the stories changed over time. It is quite conceivable that Robin Hood lived in all of the places that claim him. After all, if you were being hunted by the forces of the law, would you stay in one place all of the time?

What was life like in Robin Hood's time?

This was a time far different to the one in which we live. Travel was very difficult and most people never went far from where they were born. There were no cars. That wasn't a great problem as there were no real roads either! Electricity hadn't been invented and most people were peasants who worked the land. That meant most people were poor and worked to grow food to feed themselves and the landowners, who were very rich.

Why has the legend lasted so long?

It seems that we all like an underdog. We also have a strong sense of fair play. Therefore, although we know that Robin is an outlaw, we forgive him because it seems that he had little choice. It seems that Robin's criminal activities are there to provide a dramatic character for him rather than showing him to be a real rebel. We like him because he stands up for the weakest people in society. Despite breaking the law, he is a dashing, daring hero who does everything for the right reasons.

Reading Year 6

Text 1: Questions

> **Questions** 1–11 are about *The legend of Robin Hood* on pages **86–87**.

Marks

1. The story of Robin Hood is:

Tick **one**.

a myth. ☐

a legend. ☑

a folktale. ☐

a fable. ☐

1

2. What does *enduring* mean in the first sentence?

Tick **one**.

long lasting ☐

short lived ☐

popular ☑

unpopular ☐

1

3. Draw lines to join Robin Hood to things he might have done.

Marks

Stole from the poor
and gave to the rich.

Obeyed the law at all
times.

Robin Hood

Fought against evil.

Stole from the rich
and gave to the poor.

1

4. Find and **copy** a sentence from the first paragraph that makes us think the story of Robin Hood might not be true.

_____

_____

1

5. Read the paragraph headed **What was he like?**

Find and **copy two** different opinions of Robin Hood.

1. _Robin Hood is a popular figure_

2. _he was an outlaw and his band of followers was thought to be 100 strong._

2

Marks

6.

> How would we feel nowadays if a criminal gang of that size was hiding in Sherwood Forest?

Which word in this sentence is meant to make readers feel that the writer is talking directly to them?

_____ We _____

1

7. When do most accounts agree that Robin Hood lived?

During the time of Richard the Lionheart and King John.

1

8. Give **three** reasons, given in the text, why we cannot be sure of the facts about Robin Hood.

1. He is known as Robin Hood of Wakefield and Robin Hood of York.

2. He could have grcame from North Yorkshire or Doncaster.

3. Reasons why Robin Hood's Bay and Robin Hood airport to is named after him.

3

SCHOLASTIC SATs Tests Maths, Reading and Grammar

Marks

9. Read the paragraph headed *What was life like in Robin Hood's time?*

Why did people never go far from where they were born? Give **two** reasons.

1. <u>There were no roads</u>

2. <u>It was difficult</u>

2

10. How was life different for landowners and peasants? Give **two** differences.

1. <u>The landowners had food already · they were rich ·</u>

2. <u>The peasants worked on lands ·</u>

2

11. How do we know from the final paragraph that the writer likes Robin Hood? Give **three** examples.

1. <u>He stands up for the weakest people</u>

2. <u>He is dashing, daring hero</u>

3. <u>He does everything for the right reasons</u>

3

The happiest day I ever had

The happiest day I ever had?
When I laughed and smiled, when I was glad.

It seems to me so long ago
The day we danced in crisp cold snow;
With snowmen made in fields of white,
Watching us throughout the night.

Or a sunny day upon the beach,
With rock-pooled starfish just in reach;
And waves of foam dancing on the shore,
Daring us to go back for more.

Or watching men land on the moon,
Could it all be gone so soon?
Silver rockets in the sky,
Just memories of a time gone by.

Or dog walking in hills for miles,
Enjoying her wide doggy smiles.
Coming home encased in mud.
Yes, those days were very good.

There isn't one that is the best,
That stands out far above the rest.
I've tried and now I have to stop.
I can't choose one to come out top.

The happiest day I ever had?
When I laughed and smiled, when I was glad.
It isn't one, it isn't two.
It's every day I spend with you.

by Graham Fletcher (2016)

Marks

Questions 12–23 are about *The happiest day I ever had* on page **92**.

12. On the happiest day the author:

Tick **two**.

cried. ☐

laughed. ☑

frowned. ☐

smiled. ☑

1

13.

> The day we danced in crisp cold snow

Which word in this phrase suggests that the writer was happy?

_____ *danced* _____

1

Marks

14.

> *The day we danced in **crisp** cold snow*

Why might the cold snow have been *crisp*?

Tick **one**.

It could have been melting. ☐

It could have been roasting. ☐

It could have been frozen. ☑

It could have been going soft. ☐

1

15.

> ***rock-pooled** starfish*

What does *rock-pooled* tell us about the starfish?

The starfish wasn't in the sea.

1

Marks

16.

> *And waves of foam dancing on the shore,*
> *Daring us to go back for more.*

Find and **copy two** words that make the sea seem alive.

1. _dancing_

2. _foam_

2

17. Put a tick in the correct box to show whether each of the following statements is **true** or **false**.

	True	False
The writer watched men land on the moon.	✓	
It all happened very recently.		✓
The rockets were golden.		✓
The moon landings are just a memory now.	✓	

1

Text 2: Questions

18. Circle **one**. The writer walked the dog for:

hours.	kilometres.
days.	(miles.)

Marks

1

19.

> Coming home encased in mud.

How does this tell us that the writer walked the dog in or after bad weather?

It says that they got covered in mud.

_____

1

20. Find and **copy** a sentence that explains why the writer has stopped trying to choose his happiest day.

I can't choose one to come out top.

_____

1

21. How does the last verse link to the first one? Give **two** ways.

1. _The first and second line are both the same_

2. _____

_____

Marks

2

22. Why can the writer not choose a happiest day?

_____

_____

_____

1

23.

| *It's every day I spend with you.* |

What does this line suggest about all of the happy days in the poem?

It never ends

1

Meeting Magwitch

From **Great Expectations** by Charles Dickens

This text is taken from the beginning of **Great Expectations**. The storyteller is a young boy called Pip. He is in the churchyard, looking at the grave of his parents and his family. The other speaker is Magwitch, an escaped prisoner.

Ours was the marsh country, down by the river, within, as the river wound, twenty miles of the sea. My first most vivid and broad impression of the identity of things, seems to me to have been gained on a memorable raw afternoon towards evening. At such a time I found out for certain, that this bleak place overgrown with nettles was the churchyard; and that Philip Pirrip, late of this parish, and also Georgiana wife of the above, were dead and buried; and that Alexander, Bartholomew, Abraham, Tobias, and Roger, infant children of the aforesaid, were also dead and buried; and that the dark flat wilderness beyond the churchyard, intersected with dykes and mounds and gates, with scattered cattle feeding on it, was the marshes; and that the low leaden line beyond, was the river; and that the distant savage lair from which the wind was rushing, was the sea; and that the small bundle of shivers growing afraid of it all and beginning to cry, was Pip.

"Hold your noise!" cried a terrible voice, as a man started up from among the graves at the side of the church porch. "Keep still, you little devil, or I'll cut your throat!"

A fearful man, all in coarse grey, with a great iron on his leg. A man with no hat, and with broken shoes, and with an old rag tied round his head. A man who had been soaked in water, and smothered in mud, and lamed by stones, and cut by flints, and stung by nettles, and torn by briars; who limped, and shivered, and glared and growled; and whose teeth chattered in his head as he seized me by the chin.

"Oh! Don't cut my throat, sir," I pleaded in terror. "Pray don't do it, sir."

"Tell us your name!" said the man. "Quick!"

"Pip, sir."

"Once more," said the man, staring at me. "Give it mouth!"

"Pip. Pip, sir."

"Show us where you live," said the man. "Point out the place!"

I pointed to where our village lay, on the flat inshore among the alder trees and pollards, a mile or more from the church.

The man, after looking at me for a moment, turned me upside down, and emptied my pockets. There was nothing in them but a piece of bread. When the church came to itself — for he was so sudden and strong that he made it go head over heels before me, and I saw the steeple under my feet — when the church came to itself, I say, I was seated on a high tombstone, trembling, while he ate the bread ravenously.

"You young dog," said the man, licking his lips, "what fat cheeks you ha' got."

I believe they were fat, though I was at that time undersized for my years, and not strong.

"Darn me if I couldn't eat em," said the man, with a threatening shake of his head, "and if I han't half a mind to't!"

I earnestly expressed my hope that he wouldn't, and held tighter to the tombstone on which he had put me; partly, to keep myself upon it; partly, to keep myself from crying.

"Now lookee here!" said the man. "Where's your mother?"

"There, sir!" said I.

He started, made a short run, and stopped and looked over his shoulder.

"There, sir!" I timidly explained. "Also Georgiana. That's my mother."

"Oh!" said he, coming back. "And is that your father alonger your mother?"

"Yes, sir," said I, "him too; late of this parish."

"Ha!" he muttered then, considering. "Who d'ye live with — supposin' you're kindly let to live, which I han't made up my mind about?"

"My sister, sir — Mrs Joe Gargery — wife of Joe Gargery, the blacksmith, sir."

"Blacksmith, eh?" said he. And looked down at his leg.

After darkly looking at his leg and me several times, he came closer to my tombstone, took me by both arms, and tilted me back as far as he could hold me; so that his eyes looked most powerfully down into mine, and mine looked most helplessly up into his.

"Now lookee here," he said, "the question being whether you're to be let to live. You know what a file is?"

"Yes, sir."

"And you know what wittles is?"

"Yes, sir."

After each question he tilted me over a little more, so as to give me a greater sense of helplessness and danger.

"You get me a file." He tilted me again. "And you get me wittles." He tilted me again. "You bring 'em both to me." He tilted me again. "Or I'll have your heart and liver out." He tilted me again.

I was dreadfully frightened, and so giddy that I clung to him with both hands, and said, "If you would kindly please to let me keep upright, sir, perhaps I shouldn't be sick, and perhaps I could attend more."

He gave me a most tremendous dip and roll, so that the church jumped over its own weather cock. Then, he held me by the arms, in an upright position on the top of the stone, and went on in these fearful terms:

"You bring me, tomorrow morning early, that file and them wittles. You bring the lot to me, at that old Battery over yonder. You do it, and you never dare to say a word or dare to make a sign concerning your having seen such a person as me, or any person sumever, and you shall be let to live. You fail, or you go from my words in any partickler, no matter how small it is, and your heart and your liver shall be tore out, roasted and ate. Now, I ain't alone, as you may think I am. There's a young man hid with me, in comparison with which young man I am a Angel. That young man hears the words I speak. That young man has a secret way pecooliar to himself, of getting at a boy, and at his heart, and at his liver. It is in wain for a boy to attempt to hide himself from that young man. A boy may lock his door, may be warm in bed, may tuck himself up, may draw the clothes over his head, may think himself comfortable and safe, but that young man will softly creep and creep his way to him and tear him open. I am a-keeping that young man from harming of you at the present moment, with great difficulty. I find it wery hard to hold that young man off of your inside. Now, what do you say?"

I said that I would get him the file, and I would get him what broken bits of food I could, and I would come to him at the Battery, early in the morning.

"Say Lord strike you dead if you don't!" said the man.

Glossary

wittles (vittles) — food

Marks

Questions 24–37 are about *Meeting Magwitch* on pages **98–100**.

24. Where does Pip live?

Tick **one**.

the marsh country ☑

the churchyard ☐

the riverside ☐

the seaside ☐

1

25. Read the paragraph beginning *"Hold your noise!"*

How does the writer make Magwitch seem frightening in this paragraph? Give **two** ways.

1. _____

2. _____

2

Marks

26.

A ***fearful*** man

Circle **one** word that is closest in meaning to *fearful.*

scared	safe
(scary)	strong

1

27.

"Once more," said the man, staring at me. **"Give it mouth!"**

What does *"Give it mouth!"* mean in this text?

1

	Marks

28. Why did the church seem to go *head over heels*?

_____

_____

1

29.

> he ate the bread **ravenously**

What does the word *ravenously* tell us about how Magwitch ate the bread?

_____

_____

1

30.

> "Blacksmith, eh?" said he. And looked down at his leg.

Give **two** reasons why Magwitch might have looked down at his leg.

1. _____

2. _____

2

Text 3: Questions

31. Read the paragraph beginning *After darkly looking at his leg.*

Give **two** ways the writer makes Magwitch seem much stronger than Pip.

Marks

1. _____

2. _____

_____

2

32. Magwitch wants some *wittles.*

How does this link back to earlier in the story?

_____

_____

1

33. Which letter does Magwitch have difficulty saying?

Tick **one**.

V ☐

W ☐

X ☐

Y ☐

1

Marks

34. How does Magwitch try to make himself seem like an angel?

_____

_____

1

35. Why does the writer spell _peculiar_ as _pecooliar_?

_____

_____

1

36. Find and **copy** one way a boy may attempt to hide himself from the young man.

_____

_____

1

37. What is Pip likely to do after the end of the text? Give a reason for your answer.

_____

_____

2

End of test

Marking the test

The mark scheme is located on pages 107–110. Incorrect answers do not get a mark and no half marks should be given.

The mark scheme provides detailed examples of correct answers (although other variations/phrasings are often acceptable) and an explanation about what the answer should contain to be awarded a mark or marks.

Although the mark scheme sometimes contains alternative suggestions for correct answers, some children may find other ways of expressing a correct answer. When marking these tests, exercise judgement when assessing the accuracy or relevance of an answer and give credit for correct responses.

Answer grid

On pages 111–112 there is an answer grid for you to insert the number of marks achieved for each question. This will enable you to see which areas your child needs to practise further.

National Standard

The mark that your child gets in the test paper will be known as the 'raw score' (for example, '38' in 38/50). The raw score will be converted to a scaled score and children achieving a scaled score of 100 or more will achieve the National Standard in that subject. The DfE has introduced a conversion table to create a 'scaled score' for the tests. These 'scaled scores' enable results to be reported consistently year-on-year.

The guidance in the table below shows the marks that children need to achieve to reach the National Standard. This should be treated as a guide only, as the number of marks may vary. You can also find up-to-date information about scaled scores on our website: www.scholastic.co.uk/nationaltests

Marks achieved	Standard
0–20	Has not met the National Standard in Reading for Key Stage 2.
21–50	Has met the National Standard in Reading for Key Stage 2.

Reading mark scheme

Q	Answers	Marks
1	**Award 1 mark** for: a legend.	1
2	**Award 1 mark** for: long lasting.	1
3	**Award 1 mark** for: Robin Hood → Fought against evil. Robin Hood → Stole from the rich and gave to the poor.	1
4	**Award 1 mark** for: 'Or did he?'	1
5	**Award 2 marks** for: • He is seen as a hero or he fought for justice. • He was an outlaw. **Award 1 mark** for one of the above.	2
6	**Award 1 mark** for: 'we'.	1
7	**Award 1 mark** for: 'during the time of Richard the Lionheart and King John', or about 1190, or similar.	1
8	**Award 3 marks** for: • He lived over 800 years ago. • In those days, few people could write, so stories were passed down by word of mouth. • The stories changed over time. **Award 2 marks** for two of the above. **Award 1 mark** for one of the above.	3
9	**Award 2 marks** for any two of: • There were no cars. • There were no real roads. • Travel was very difficult. **Award 1 mark** for one of the above.	2
10	**Award 2 marks** for: • Peasants were poor or peasants worked the land, but landowners were rich. • Peasants grew their own food and food for the landowners, but landowners did not have to grow their own food. **Award 1 mark** for one of the above.	2

Q	Answers	Marks
11	**Award 3 marks** for any three of: • We all like an underdog. • The writer forgives him for being an outlaw. • The writer understands that Robin Hood had little choice. • Robin Hood stands up for the weakest in society. • Robin Hood is a dashing, daring hero. • Robin Hood did everything for the right reasons. **Award 2 marks** for any two of the above. **Award 1 mark** for one of the above.	3
12	**Award 1 mark** for both correct: • laughed. • smiled.	1
13	**Award 1 mark** for: 'danced'.	1
14	**Award 1 mark** for: It could have been frozen.	1
15	**Award 1 mark** for answers that show understanding of the starfish being in rock pools.	1
16	**Award 2 marks** for: • dancing. • daring. **Award 1 mark** for one of the above.	2
17	**Award 1 mark** for all correct:	1

Q17 table:

	True	False
The writer watched men land on the moon.	✓	
It all happened very recently.		✓
The rockets were golden.		✓
The moon landings are just a memory now.	✓	

Q	Answers	Marks
18	**Award 1 mark** for: miles.	1
19	**Award 1 mark** for answers that explain that mud is caused by rain.	1
20	**Award 1 mark** for: 'I can't choose one to come out top.' or 'There isn't one that is the best, That stands out far above the rest.'	1
21	**Award 2 marks** for: • The first two lines are repeated at the end. • The last verse reminds the reader of the first question and answers it. **Award 1 mark** for one of the above.	2
22	**Award 1 mark** for: There wasn't just one day, or there were lots of happiest days.	1
23	**Award 1 mark** for answers that suggest the days were spent with 'you', or similar.	1
24	**Award 1 mark** for: the marsh country.	1

Q	Answers	Marks
25	**Award 2 marks** for two of: • Magwitch seems to appear from nowhere, or similar. • He has a 'terrible voice'. • He threatens to cut Pip's throat/murder Pip, or similar. **Award 1 mark** for one of the above.	2
26	**Award 1 mark** for: scary.	1
27	**Award 1 mark** for: 'Say it', 'say it louder', or similar.	1
28	**Award 1 mark** for: Magwitch had turned Pip upside down.	1
29	**Award 1 mark** for: he ate it hungrily, quickly, or similar.	1
30	**Award 2 marks** for any two of: • He had an 'iron' on his leg. • The blacksmith might be able to remove the iron from his leg. • He might be able to use the blacksmith's tools to remove the iron from his leg. **Award 1 mark** for one of the above.	2
31	**Award 2 marks** for any two of: • Magwitch tilted Pip backwards. • Magwitch's eyes were powerful. • Pip looked helplessly at Magwitch. • The position of both of them – Magwitch looked 'down' at Pip/Pip looked 'up' at Magwitch. **Award 1 mark** for one of the above.	2
32	**Award 1 mark** for either of: • He was hungry. • He ate Pip's bread 'ravenously'.	1
33	**Award 1 mark** for: V.	1
34	**Award 1 mark** for any of: • He compares himself to the young man. • He says the young man is much worse than he is. • He says he is protecting Pip by stopping the young man killing him.	1
35	**Award 1 mark** for answers that show understanding of it being the way Magwitch says it, or similar.	1
36	**Award 1 mark** for any of the following: • lock his door. • be warm in bed. • tuck himself up. • draw the clothes over his head.	1

Q	Answers	Marks
37	**Award 2 marks** for reasonable answers that include an explanation. Possible responses include: • Bring the file and wittles because he believes that Magwitch and/or the young man will kill him if he doesn't, or similar. • Tell the blacksmith or his sister about Magwitch because he believes they will protect him, or similar. **Award 1 mark** for reasonable answers that do not include an explanation.	2
	Total	**50**

Q	Focus	Possible marks	Actual marks
1	Information/key details	1	
2	Meanings of words	1	
3	Information/key details	1	
4	Meanings of words	1	
5	Information/key details	2	
6	Identifying/explaining choice of words and phrases	1	
7	Information/key details	1	
8	Information/key details	3	
9	Information/key details	2	
10	Making comparisons	2	
11	Making inferences	3	
12	Information/key details	1	
13	Making inferences	1	
14	Meanings of words	1	
15	Meanings of words	1	
16	Meanings of words	2	
17	Information/key details	1	
18	Information/key details	1	
19	Making inferences	1	
20	Information/key details	1	
21	Identifying/explaining how information is related	2	
22	Making inferences	1	
23	Summarise	1	

Reading Year 6

Answer grid

Q	Focus	Possible marks	Actual marks
24	Information/key details	1	
25	Making inferences	2	
26	Meanings of words	1	
27	Meanings of words	1	
28	Making inferences	1	
29	Meanings of words	1	
30	Making inferences	2	
31	Making inferences	2	
32	Identifying/explaining how information is related	1	
33	Information/key details	1	
34	Making inferences	1	
35	Identifying/explaining choice of words and phrases	1	
36	Information/key details	1	
37	Predicting	2	
	Total	**50**	

Test coverage

Children will need to be able to:

- Give and explain meanings of words.
- Retrieve and write down key details.
- Summarise main ideas from more than one paragraph.
- Make inferences from the text and use details to explain their thoughts about them.
- Predict what might happen.
- Identify and explain how information is organised.
- Show how writers use language to create an effect.
- Make comparisons.

The answer grid on pages 111–112 lists the coverage of each question. Use this information to identify any areas that your child finds difficult and to emphasise the skills of inference and retrieval, which are assigned the most marks.

There are different types of answer:

- **Selected answers:** children may be required to choose an option from a list; draw lines to match answers; circle or tick a correct answer. Usually 1 mark will be awarded.
- **Short answers:** children will need to write a phrase or use information from the text. Usually 1–2 marks will be awarded.
- **Longer answers:** children will usually need to write more than one sentence using information from the text. Up to 3 marks will be awarded.

Notes

3

GRAMMAR

CONTENTS

Grammar, Punctuation and Spelling Year 6

Advice for parents and carers

In the run up to the National Tests, provide your child with lots of support and practice.

Before the test:

- Read through Paper 1, so that you know what your child will be doing. You could even try to complete it yourself, so you know how difficult it is.

- Let your child take both papers (Grammar and Punctuation, and Spelling) under examination conditions (45 minutes for Grammar and Punctuation questions; approximately 15 minutes for Spelling). Do not provide any help.

- Go through the answers and mark the test together. Talk about which parts of the test your child found difficult.

- Make a list of areas for further revision and encourage your child to practise these areas for two hours each week.

General preparation for the practice tests:

- Make sure that you allow your child to take the practice test in a quiet environment with minimal distractions.

- Make sure your child has a flat surface to work on with plenty of space to spread out, and good light.

- Emphasise the importance of reading and re-reading a question and encourage your child to underline or circle any important information.

In the run up to the test:

- Revise and practise on a regular basis.
- Take the practice test.
- Mark it with an adult and discuss questions that you found difficult. Make a list of areas for future revision.
- Spend at least two hours each week practising.
- Focus on the areas you are least confident in so that you can improve.

Just before the test:

- Get a good night's sleep and eat a wholesome breakfast.
- Be on time for school.
- Have all the necessary materials.
- Avoid stressful situations before the test.

During the test:

- Read the questions carefully. Then read them again.
- Circle or underline any important information in the question.
- If you're struggling with a question, move on and return to it at the end.
- Write as clearly as you can.
- Use every minute of the test time. If you've finished, check your answers.

Paper 1: Questions

Marks

1. Underline the **verbs** in this sentence.

While the elephants <u>crashed</u> through the trees, monkeys <u>chattered</u> and <u>scampered</u> out of the way.

1

2. Write a **question** starting with <u>who</u>.

Who <u>are you?</u>

1

3. Draw lines to the correct labels for each sentence.

Finish your homework.	Question
I have finished my homework.	Exclamation
Have you finished your homework?	Statement
What great homework you have done!	Command

1

Marks

4. Draw lines to join the words to the correct **contraction**.

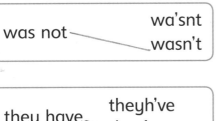

was not   wa'snt / wasn't

could not   could'nt / couldn't

they have   theyh've / they've

where is   where's / wheres'

1

5. Underline the **main clause** in this sentence.

In the event of a fire, <u>please assemble in the car park.</u>

1

6. Circle the best **synonym** to replace the word in bold.

The **persuasive** salesman almost sold us a car.

Circle **one**.

talkative	convincing	attractive

1

7. Underline the **noun phrase** in the sentence below.

The children ran to the track to <u>watch</u> the green steam train puff by.

1

Marks

8. Rewrite the sentence in **Standard English**.

I were going to the party but they cancels it.

I was going to the party but they cancelled it.

1

9. Use the **prefixes** to make new words. Use each prefix once.

auto	il	mis	de

motivate ⟶ _demotivate_

legal ⟶ _illegal_

fortune ⟶ _misfortune_

biography ⟶ _autobiography_

1

10. Draw lines to match each sentence with the best **punctuation**.

Sentence   **Punctuation**

| How terrible that is | — | . |

| How could they watch such terrible things | | ! |

| I do not know how such terrible things could happen | | ? |

1

Marks

11. Change the underlined words to **plurals**.

The <u>baby</u> drank the <u>bottle</u> of milk.

| babies | bottles |

1

12. Underline the **pronouns** in these sentences.

The car was <u>theirs</u> but was due to be sold.

The groom, <u>who</u> was wearing a burgundy waistcoat, smiled happily.

1

13. For each of these words, write another word from the same **word family**.

act   _acting_

care   _careful_

help   _helper_

1

Marks

14. Underline **all** the **adverbs**.

The weather forecaster <u>gloomily</u> said that we may perhaps have snow later.

1

15. Rewrite this sentence in the **present progressive form**.

They revised all morning for their maths examination.

<u>They did revision all morning for their maths examinatition.</u>

1

16. Complete the sentences below using either <u>I</u> or <u>me</u>.

I was hoping Katie would pick <u>me</u> for the team.

Katie and <u>I</u> were picked up from school, after the game.

1

17. Underline the word or words that make the sentence below a **question**.

That <u>was</u> <u>a</u> <u>fantastic</u> <u>concert</u>, wasn't <u>it</u>?

1

Marks

18. This sentence has a **main clause** and an **adverbial** in it.

After the concert, it took a long time to leave the arena.

a. Tick the **main clause**.

Tick **one**.

After the concert,	☐
it took a long time	☐
it took a long time to leave the arena	☑

1

b. Tick the **adverbial**.

Tick **one**.

After the concert,	☑
it took a long time	☐
it took a long time to leave the arena	☐

1

19. Insert an **apostrophe** into the correct place in each sentence.

Shakespeare's plays are performed in theatres throughout the world.

Theatre companies' performances of Shakespearean plays vary enormously.

1

Paper 1: Questions

20. Draw a line to match the beginning of the sentence to the correct ending.

Marks

can be used to modify verbs.

join ideas in different sentences.

Adverbs

separate items in a list.

give additional information.

1

21. a. Underline the **subject** of this sentence.

We made a huge snowman.

1

b. Underline the **object** of this sentence.

Josh watched the snow falling silently.

1

22. Insert three **apostrophes** in the sentences below.

We've had a fantastic evening at their house. It wasn't boring at all – we couldn't have asked for better company.

1

23. Which of these does not always need a **capital letter**?

Tick **one**.

the name of a city ☐

a day of the week ☐

a person's name ☐

a personal pronoun ☑

Marks

1

---

24. Replace the underlined words in each sentence with a **pronoun**.

We camped in <u>a caravan</u> last Easter.

↓

there

We watched <u>the planes</u> zooming overhead.

↓

them

1

---

25. Choose the best **determiners** to complete the sentence.

a   an

_*An*_ agile deer jumped in front of _*a*_ red car.

1

Marks

26. Add the missing **commas** to the sentence.

The hotel's facilities included a swimming pool, a gym, a playroom and a children's club.

1

27. In the sentence below, Jack walked the dog <u>before</u> drying it. Complete the sentence with the correct **verb form**.

Although Jack __*had*__ walked the dog, he still needed to dry it.

1

28. Which of the events below is **most** likely to happen?

Tick **one**.

We might see a meteor shower. ☑

We should see a meteor shower. ☐

We will see a meteor shower. ☐

We could see a meteor shower. ☐

1

Marks

29. Underline the **relative clause** in the sentence below.

The gymnast, <u>whose hard work had won her the gold</u> <u>medal,</u> was thrilled.

1

30. Choose the best **subordinating conjunctions** to complete the sentences.

> although   when   because

We asked the usher ___*when*___ the concert was due to finish.

I cannot play in the football match tonight

___*because*___ I have broken my leg.

1

31. Underline the **prepositions** in the sentences below.

I haven't seen you <u>since</u> August.

They enjoy a walk <u>after</u> their lunch.

He snuggled down <u>under</u> the warm duvet.

1

32. Insert a **comma** and a **semi-colon** in the sentence below, to clarify its meaning.

Despite the appalling weather, the outdoor activities continued this caused; some parents great anxiety.

Marks

1

---

33. The sentence below is written in the **passive voice**.

The stick was chased by the enthusiastic young Labrador.

Which of the sentences below are written in the **active voice**?

Tick **two**.

The enthusiastic young Labrador chased the stick. ✓

The stick was being chased enthusiastically. ☐

The young Labrador was chased by the stick. ☐

Enthusiastically, the young Labrador chased the stick. ☐

1

Marks

34. Tick one box in each row to show the **types of adverb**.

	Adverb of time	Adverb of possibility	Adverb of place
somewhere			✓
certainly		✓	
yesterday	✓		

1

35. Choose the correct **relative pronoun** for each sentence.

> that   which

The gift _that_ I was hoping for was a pencil case.

The hotel, _which_ was next to the river, was lovely.

1

36. Add these **suffixes** to the root words below to make **nouns**. You may need to change the endings.

> ence   acy   ance

accurate ⟶ _acy_ ⟶ _accuratacy_

acquaint ⟶ _ence_ ⟶ _acquaintence_

interfere ⟶ _ance_ ⟶ _interferance_

1

37. Tick one box in each row to show whether the word <u>before</u> is used as a **subordinating conjunction** or as a **preposition**.

Marks

Sentence	<u>before</u> used as a subordinating conjunction	<u>before</u> used as a preposition
Asha read her book <u>before</u> going to bed.		✓
I need to arrive <u>before</u> Wednesday.	✓	
The Jones family expect to go on holiday <u>before</u> the end of August.	✓	

1

38. Which option completes the sentence below, so that it uses the **subjunctive mood**?

I would enjoy it if I _____ able to spend a night here.

Tick **one**.

were ☐

could be ☐

might be ☐

was ✓

1

SCHOLASTIC SATs Tests Maths, Reading and Grammar

39. Tick one box to show the correct place to insert a **comma** in the sentence below.

Before the party can we discuss what we will need?

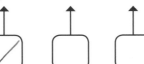 

Marks

1

---

40. Which of the sentences below uses **dashes** correctly?

Tick **one**.

The dress was stunning – very delicate lace – it looked amazing on her.

The dress was – stunning very delicate lace – it looked amazing on her.

The dress – was stunning – very delicate lace it looked amazing on her.

The dress was stunning very delicate lace – it looked amazing – on her.

1

41. a. Draw lines to join the labels to the correct places in the text.

Marks

Our trip

Mum and Dad had promised us a special day out. When the day finally came, we were very excited. It was a long journey but eventually we arrived at Bilton Towers, our favourite theme park. After a long queue to buy tickets, we were in!

Amazing rides!

As we walked through the turnstiles, we could see some amazing rides: Swinging Pirate Boats; the Big Cave Rollercoaster and the Jolly Roger Scary Train.

Paragraph 1

Paragraph 2

Heading

Subheading

1

b. This text is split into two **paragraphs** because:

Tick **one**.

it is about two places. ☑

it was lots of fun. ☐

it is about the trip and then about what was at the theme park. ☐

it is about being excited and being frightened. ☐

1

Marks

42. <u>Eventually</u>, we arrived at the seaside, where the sun was shining.

In the sentence above, <u>eventually</u> is used as:

Circle **one**.

(an adverb)   (an adjective)

(a preposition)   (a determiner)

1

43. <u>As</u> the sun went down, we watched an owl swoop under the trees.

The word <u>as</u> is used to introduce:

Tick **one**.

a noun phrase.   ☐

a main clause.   ☐

a subordinating conjunction.   ☐

an adverbial phrase.   ☑

1

Marks

44. The phrase below would be clearer with a **hyphen**.

sugar free fruit drink

Which of the phrases below uses a hyphen correctly?

Tick **one**.

sugar free-fruit drink ☐

sugar-free fruit drink ☑

sugar free fruit-drink ☐

1

45. Add a different **suffix** to each word to create new words. You may need to change the root word.

ate   ise   ity

critic   ⟶   *criticise*

consider   ⟶   *considerate*

acid   ⟶   *acidity*

1

46. Add a **prefix** to change the word <u>familiar</u> into its **antonym**.

familiar   ⟶   *unfamiliar*

1

47. The sentence below would be clearer with **semi-colons**.

Marks

The recipe requires: 200g of self-raising flour, sifted, 200g of unsalted butter, melted, four eggs, whisked, 200g of caster sugar and a teaspoon of vanilla essence.

Which of the sentences below uses **semi-colons** correctly?

Tick **one**.

The recipe requires: 200g; of self-raising flour, sifted, 200g; of unsalted butter, melted, four eggs, whisked, 200g; of caster sugar and a teaspoon of vanilla essence. ☐

The recipe requires: 200g of self-raising flour, sifted; 200g of unsalted butter, melted; four eggs, whisked; 200g of caster sugar and a teaspoon of vanilla essence. ☑

The recipe requires: 200g of self-raising flour; sifted, 200g of unsalted butter; melted, four eggs; whisked, 200g of caster sugar and a teaspoon of vanilla essence. ☐

The recipe requires: 200g of self-raising flour, sifted, 200g of unsalted butter, melted, four eggs, whisked, 200g of caster sugar; and a teaspoon of vanilla essence. ☐

1

End of paper

Paper 2: Spelling

Instructions

- Your **spelling** will be tested in this paper.

- **20 short sentences** will be read aloud to you. A single word has been missed out of each sentence and you need to write this in the space provided.

- **You will hear each word three times.** The word will be said once, then read within a sentence and then repeated a third time. You should write the spelling in the space provided.

- All 20 sentences will be read again at the end, when you will be able to make any changes you wish to what you have written down.

- This paper should take approximately **15 minutes** to complete, although you will be allowed as much time as you need to complete the test.

1. The train station was very _____.

2. They were amazed by the _____ of the weightlifter.

3. We made a _____ effort to buy a suitable present for her birthday.

4. We use a pair of compasses to draw a _____.

5. The announcement was met with _____.

6. The _____ helped with the symptoms of the cold.

7. The rival football supporters were _____ inside the stadium.

8. I forgot to _____ that we will be visiting your aunt and uncle.

9. The cricket team's _____ was announced in the school hall.

10. The _____ of the audience led to an encore.

Grammar, Punctuation and Spelling Year 6

Paper 2: Spelling

11. The _____ prize for literacy was won by Aiden.

12. We watched as the _____ flashed over the houses.

13. The class clapped out the _____ started by the teacher.

14. There was no _____ when our children met the French exchange children.

15. During maths we had to sort shapes into each _____.

16. You will need a parent's _____ to say you are able to go on the trip.

17. The efforts of the local community have improved the _____.

18. A full moon _____ each month.

19. As we walked through the field, we could see the cow _____ trying to reach her calf.

20. We were sent a detailed _____ of how to get to the cottage.

End of paper

SCHOLASTIC   SATs Tests Maths, Reading and Grammar

Marking Paper 1

The mark scheme for this paper is located on pages 141–144.
Most of the questions have right or wrong answers. However, there are some open-ended questions that require your child's input. For these questions, example answers have been provided. However, they are not exhaustive and alternatives are appropriate, so a certain degree of interpretation will be needed.

Question type	Accept	Do not accept
Tick boxes	Clear unambiguous marks.	Responses where more boxes have been ticked than required.
Circling or underlining	Clear unambiguous indication of the correct answer – including a box.	Responses where more than the required number of words have been circled or underlined. Responses where the correct answer is circled or underlined, together with surrounding words. Answers in which less than half of the required word is circled or underlined.
Drawing lines	Lines that do not touch the boxes, provided the intention is clear.	Multiple lines drawn to or from the same box (unless a requirement of the question).
Labelling parts of speech	Clear labels, whether they use the full vocabulary required by the question or an unambiguous abbreviation.	Ambiguity in labelling such as the use of 'CN' when asked to identify collective nouns and common nouns.
Punctuation	Punctuation that is clear, unambiguous and recognisable as the required punctuation mark.	Punctuation that is ambiguous, for example if it is unclear whether the mark is a comma or full stop.
Spelling	Where no specific mark scheme guidance is given, incorrect spellings of the correct response should be accepted.	Correct spelling is generally required for questions assessing contracted forms, plurals, verb tenses, prefixes and suffixes.

Marking the test

Marking Paper 2

- If more than one attempt is made to spell a word, it must be clear which version the child wishes to be marked.

- Spellings can be written in upper or lower case, or a mixture of the two.

- If a word has been written with the correct sequence of letters but they have been separated into clearly divided components, with or without a dash, the mark is not awarded.

- If a word has been written with the correct sequence of letters but an apostrophe or hyphen has been inserted, the mark is not awarded.

- Any acceptable British English spelling can be marked as correct. For example, *organise* or *organize*.

Marks table

On pages 148–149, there are answer grids for you to insert the number of marks achieved for each question. This will enable you to see which areas your child needs to practise further.

National Standard

The mark that your child gets in the test paper will be known as the 'raw score' (for example, '38' in 38/50). The raw score will be converted to a scaled score and children achieving a scaled score of 100 or more will achieve the National Standard in that subject. The DfE has introduced a conversion table to create a 'scaled score' for the test. These 'scaled scores' will enable results to be reported consistently year-on-year.

The guidance in the table below shows the marks that children need to achieve to reach the National Standard. This should be treated as a guide only, as the number of marks may vary. You can also find up-to-date information about scaled scores on our website: www.scholastic.co.uk/nationaltests

Marks achieved	Standard
0–42	Has not met the National Standard in Grammar, Punctuation and Spelling for Key Stage 2.
43–70	Has met the National Standard in Grammar, Punctuation and Spelling for Key Stage 2.

Q	Answers	Marks
1	While the elephants <u>crashed</u> through the trees, monkeys <u>chattered</u> and <u>scampered</u> out of the way.	1
2	**Accept** any question starting with 'who' and ending with a question mark. For example: Who has finished their work?	1
3	Finish your homework. → Command I have finished my homework. → Statement Have you finished your homework? → Question What great homework you have done! → Exclamation	1
4	was not → wasn't they have → they've could not → couldn't where is → where's	1
5	In the event of a fire, <u>please assemble in the car park</u>.	1
6	convincing	1
7	The children ran to the track to watch the <u>green steam train</u> puff by. **Also accept** answers where <u>the</u> is underlined.	1
8	I was going to the party but they cancelled it.	1
9	demotivate, illegal, misfortune, autobiography	1
10	How terrible that is → ! How could they watch such terrible things → ? I do not know how such terrible things could happen → .	1
11	babies, bottles	1
12	The car was <u>theirs</u> but was due to be sold. The groom, <u>who</u> was wearing a burgundy waistcoat, smiled happily.	1

Q	Answers	Marks
13	**Accept** any words that belong to the word families below (one word per family required). For example:	1

act	care	help
acts (or other present or past tense forms of the verb)	cares (or other present or past tense forms of the verb)	helps (or other present or past tense forms of the verb)
action	careful	helper
active	carefully	helping
activity	careless	helpful
actor	carelessness	helpfully
counteract	caretaker	helpless
enact	childcare	helplessness
inactivity	uncaring	unhelpful

Q	Answers	Marks
14	The weather forecaster <u>gloomily</u> said that we may <u>perhaps</u> have snow <u>later</u>.	1
15	They are revising all morning for their maths examination.	1
16	I was hoping Katie would pick **me** for the team. Katie and **I** were picked up from school, after the game.	1
17	That was a fantastic concert, <u>wasn't it</u>? **Also accept** responses that underline the comma and/or the question mark in addition to the correct words.	1
18	**a.** it took a long time to leave the arena	1
	b. After the concert,	1
19	Shakespeare's plays are performed in theatres throughout the world. Theatre companies' performances of Shakespearean plays vary enormously.	1
20		1

Adverbs → can be used to modify verbs.

join ideas in different sentences.

separate items in a list.

give additional information.

Q	Answers	Marks
21	**a.** <u>We</u> made a huge snowman.	1
	b. Josh watched <u>the snow</u> falling silently.	1
22	We've had a fantastic evening at their house. It wasn't boring at all – we couldn't have asked for better company.	1
23	a personal pronoun	1
24	We camped in <u>it</u> last Easter. or We camped in <u>there</u> last Easter. We watched <u>them</u> zooming overhead.	1
25	**An** agile deer jumped in front of **a** red car.	1

Q	Answers	Marks
26	The hotel's facilities included a swimming pool**,** a gym**,** a playroom and a children's club.	I
27	Although Jack **had** walked the dog, he still needed to dry it.	I
28	We will see a meteor shower.	I
29	The gymnast, <u>whose hard work had won her the gold medal</u>, was thrilled.	I
30	We asked the usher **when** the concert was due to finish. I cannot play in the football match tonight **because** I have broken my leg.	I
31	I haven't seen you <u>since</u> August. They enjoy a walk <u>after</u> their lunch. He snuggled down <u>under</u> the warm duvet.	I
32	Despite the appalling weather**,** the outdoor activities continued**;** this caused some parents great anxiety.	I
33	The enthusiastic young Labrador chased the stick. Enthusiastically, the young Labrador chased the stick.	I

34		Adverb of time	Adverb of possibility	Adverb of place	I
	somewhere			✓	
	certainly		✓		
	yesterday	✓			

35	The gift **that** I was hoping for was a pencil case. The hotel, **which** was next to the river, was lovely.	I
36	accuracy, acquaintance, interference	I

37	Sentence	before used as a subordinating conjunction	before used as a preposition	I
	Asha read her book <u>before</u> going to bed.	✓		
	I need to arrive <u>before</u> Wednesday.		✓	
	The Jones family expect to go on holiday <u>before</u> the end of August.		✓	

38	were	I
39	Before the party**,** can we discuss what we will need?	I
40	The dress was stunning – very delicate lace – it looked amazing on her.	I

Q	Answers	Marks
41	**a.** Paragraph 1 – Mum and Dad had promised... Paragraph 2 – As we walked... Heading – Our trip Subheading – Amazing rides!	1
	b. It is about the trip and then about what was at the theme park.	1
42	an adverb	1
43	an adverbial phrase.	1
44	sugar-free fruit drink	1
45	criticise, considerate, acidity	1
46	unfamiliar	1
47	The recipe requires: 200g of self-raising flour, sifted; 200g of unsalted butter, melted; four eggs, whisked; 200g of caster sugar and a teaspoon of vanilla essence.	1
	Total	**50**

■SCHOLASTIC   SATs Tests Maths, Reading and Grammar

Spelling transcript

Notes for conducting the spelling test

The paper should take approximately **15 minutes** to complete, although you should allow your child as much time as they need to complete it.

Read the instructions below to your child.

Listen carefully to the instructions I am going to give you.

I am going to read 20 sentences to you. Each sentence has a word missing on your answer page. You should listen carefully to the missing word and fill this in, making sure you spell it correctly.

I will read the word, then the word within a sentence and then repeat the word a third time.

Do you have any questions?

Then read the spellings as follows:

1. Give the spelling number.

2. Say 'The word is...'.

3. Read the context sentence.

4. Repeat 'The word is...'.

Leave at least a 12-second gap between spellings.

At the end, re-read all 20 questions. Then say: *This is the end of the test; please put down your pen or pencil.*

Each correct answer should be awarded **1 mark**. For more information on marking this paper, please refer to page 140.

Spelling one: the word is **busy**.

The train station was very **busy**.

The word is **busy**.

Spelling two: the word is **strength**.

They were amazed by the **strength** of the weightlifter.

The word is **strength**.

Spelling three: the word is **special**.

We made a **special** effort to buy a suitable present for her birthday.

The word is **special**.

Spelling four: the word is **circle**.

We use a pair of compasses to draw a **circle**.

The word is **circle**.

Spelling five: the word is **disbelief**.

The announcement was met with **disbelief**.

The word is **disbelief**.

Spelling six: the word is **medicine**.

The **medicine** helped with the symptoms of the cold.

The word is **medicine**.

Spelling seven: the word is **separated**.

The rival football supporters were **separated** inside the stadium.

The word is **separated**.

Spelling eight: the word is **mention**.

I forgot to **mention** that we will be visiting your aunt and uncle.

The word is **mention**.

Spelling nine: the word is **achievement**.

The cricket team's **achievement** was announced in the school hall.

The word is **achievement**.

Spelling ten: the word is **appreciation**.

The **appreciation** of the audience led to an encore.

The word is **appreciation**.

Spelling eleven: the word is **individual**.

The **individual** prize for literacy was won by Aiden.

The word is **individual**.

Spelling twelve: the word is **lightning**.

We watched as the **lightning** flashed over the houses.

The word is **lightning**.

Spelling thirteen: the word is **rhythm**.

The class clapped out the **rhythm** started by the teacher.

The word is **rhythm**.

Spelling fourteen: the word is **awkwardness**.

There was no **awkwardness** when our children met the French exchange children.

The word is **awkwardness**.

Spelling fifteen: the word is **category**.

During maths we had to sort shapes into each **category**.

The word is **category**.

Spelling sixteen: the word is **signature**.

You will need a parent's **signature** to say you are able to go on the trip.

The word is **signature**.

Spelling seventeen: the word is **neighbourhood**.

The efforts of the local community have improved the **neighbourhood**.

The word is **neighbourhood**.

Spelling eighteen: the word is **occurs**.

A full moon **occurs** each month.

The word is **occurs**.

Spelling nineteen: the word is **desperately**.

As we walked through the field, we could see the cow **desperately** trying to reach her calf.

The word is **desperately**.

Spelling twenty: the word is **explanation**.

We were sent a detailed **explanation** of how to get to the cottage.

The word is **explanation**.

Paper 1: Answer grid

Q	Focus	Possible marks	Actual marks
1	Grammar: verbs	1	
2	Grammar: questions	1	
3	Grammar: questions, statements, exclamations, commands	1	
4	Punctuation: apostrophes	1	
5	Grammar: sentences and clauses	1	
6	Vocabulary: synonyms and antonyms	1	
7	Grammar: noun phrases	1	
8	Grammar: Standard English	1	
9	Vocabulary: prefixes	1	
10	Punctuation: question marks, exclamation marks, full stops Grammar: questions, statements, exclamations, commands	1	
11	Vocabulary: suffixes	1	
12	Grammar: pronouns	1	
13	Vocabulary: word families	1	
14	Grammar: adverbs	1	
15	Grammar: present and past progressive	1	
16	Grammar: pronouns	1	
17	Grammar: questions	1	
18	Grammar: main clauses and fronted adverbials	2	
19	Punctuation: apostrophes	1	
20	Grammar: adverbs	1	
21	Grammar: subject and object	2	
22	Punctuation: apostrophes	1	
23	Punctuation: capital letters	1	
24	Grammar: pronouns	1	
25	Grammar: determiners	1	

Paper 1 and Paper 2 : Answer grid

Q	Focus	Possible marks	Actual marks
26	Punctuation: commas	1	
27	Grammar: verbs in the perfect form	1	
28	Grammar: modal verbs	1	
29	Grammar: relative clauses	1	
30	Grammar: subordinating conjunctions and subordinate clauses	1	
31	Grammar: prepositions	1	
32	Punctuation: commas to clarify meaning, semi-colons	1	
33	Grammar: passive and active	1	
34	Grammar: adverbs	1	
35	Grammar: relative pronouns	1	
36	Vocabulary: suffixes	1	
37	Grammar: subordinating conjunctions and subordinate clauses, prepositions	1	
38	Grammar: subjunctive verb forms	1	
39	Punctuation: commas after fronted adverbials	1	
40	Punctuation: punctuation for parenthesis	1	
41	Punctuation: paragraphs, headings	2	
42	Grammar: adverbs	1	
43	Grammar: adverbials	1	
44	Punctuation: hyphens	1	
45	Vocabulary: suffixes	1	
46	Vocabulary: prefixes, synonyms and antonyms	1	
47	Punctuation: semi-colons	1	
1–20	Spelling	20	
	Total	70	

Grammar, Punctuation and Spelling Year 6

Test coverage

Paper 1: Grammar and Punctuation

Your child will need to be familiar with and be able to demonstrate use of the following, including correct use of all grammatical terms.

	Content
Grammatical words and word classes	Nouns
	Verbs
	Adjectives
	Conjunctions
	Pronouns Possessive pronouns Relative pronouns
	Adverbs Adverbials Fronted adverbials
	Prepositions
	Determiners
	Subjects Objects
Functions of sentences	Statements Questions Exclamations Commands
Combining words, phrases and clauses	Sentences Clauses
	Noun phrases
	Co-ordinating conjunctions Subordinating conjunctions Subordinate clauses
Verb forms, tense and consistency	Simple past and simple present tense Verbs in the perfect form Modal verbs Present and past progressive tense Tense consistency
	Subjunctive verb forms Passive Active

■SCHOLASTIC SATs Tests Maths, Reading and Grammar

	Content
Punctuation	Capital letters
	Full stops
	Question marks
	Exclamation marks
	Commas in lists
	Commas to clarify meaning
	Commas after fronted adverbials
	Inverted commas
	Apostrophes for contraction
	Apostrophes for possession
	Punctuation for parenthesis
	Colons
	Semi-colons
	Single dashes
	Hyphens
	Bullet points
Vocabulary	Synonyms
	Antonyms
	Prefixes
	Suffixes
	Word families
Standard English and formality	Standard English
	Formal and informal vocabulary
	Formal and informal structures
	The subjunctive
Partially assessed	Paragraphs
	Headings
	Subheadings